Baptism: How Important Is It?

Baptism: How Important Is It?

Henry M. Morris III

ACCENT BOOKS
Denver, Colorado

ACCENT BOOKS
A division of Accent-B/P Publications, Inc.
12100 W. Sixth Avenue
P.O. Box 15337
Denver, Colorado 80215

Copyright © 1978 Accent-B/P Publications, Inc.
Printed in U.S.A.

Library of Congress Catalog Number: 77-87954

ISBN 0-916406-72-5

CONTENTS

Chapter 1

Is Baptism Important?

Do you know what the Bible says about baptism? Most folks don't. As a matter of fact, there are a number of churches that teach their people that baptism is a matter of personal preference. That is, it doesn't matter whether you are baptized or not—whether you are sprinkled or put under the water—it's the thought that counts. Well, if the Bible does *not* teach anything specific about the *method* of baptism, or if there are no specific instructions about *who* is to be baptized, then it really doesn't matter after all. So let's find out.

Many Protestant denominations teach that the sprinkling of infants is the *best* way to baptize, although some of them will allow their members to be immersed if asked. All of these churches base their practice on two main points: that baptism is the New Testament seal of the covenant, as circumcision was for the Old Testament, and that the majority of churches have practiced sprinkling for centuries. Are they right? If they are, does it mean churches practicing baptism by immersing people in water are too fussy?

Another problem: some churches insist upon trine immersion; that is, each candidate is immersed three times. They base that practice on Matthew 28:19 where our Lord says we are to baptize "in the name of the Father, and of the Son, and of the Holy Ghost." And, even among these churches, some baptize three times face downward, and others three times face upward. Is that unnecessary, or more correct? Which is right? Face up, or face down? What does the Bible say? Do you know?

Well, if you are like most people, you probably feel that your church is right, and you are not sure why the other churches do it differently. However, you will defend their right to do whatever they feel is right . . .as long as they believe the Bible and preach the gospel. The only problem with that is . . . the Bible doesn't support that way of looking at baptism or anything else that pertains to what we should believe and what we should do. You see, every word in Scripture is important. What the Bible teaches about baptism is absolute. It is not left to the preferences of any group to determine the meaning of baptism or how it should be administered. Rather, we must search the Word of God to learn what baptism means and how it should be administered, for we are accountable to God to obey what He commands.

Well, can we expect to come to the Bible and find clear instructions about baptism? I believe so, for the Lord Jesus would not want us to be in the dark about how to obey His command to baptize (Matthew 28:19). He put too much stock in each word of the Scriptures for Him to tolerate the breaking of even the "least" commandment (Matthew 5:19). Also, the Apostle Peter tells us that the Word of God gives us "all things that pertain unto life and godliness" (II Peter 1:3). Moses told us in Deuteronomy 29:29 that "the secret things belong unto the Lord our God: but those things which are revealed belong unto us and to our children forever, that we may do all the words of this law."

If words mean anything, the Bible ought to tell us both *how* and *who* to baptize. Besides that, there ought to be clear evidence in the lives of the early churches that would verify what was believed and practiced by those Christians who were right on the heels of the apostles. This study is going to take you through the "hard" data of history, the language of the Bible, and those verses that have an effect on the ordinance practiced by the New Testament church. When we're through, you ought to *know* the answers to the puzzling questions raised a few paragraphs back. God is *not* the author of confusion. We can know what the right teaching is . . . *if* we are willing to obey it when we find it (John 7:17).

The weight of historical evidence cannot be given as much place as either Biblical or linguistic evidence, but it certainly can provide a significant push to get the ball rolling. As we concern ourselves with the historical background of the ordinance of baptism we need to look at two major areas. The first area has to answer the question of origin, development, and reason for the change from immersion to sprinkling. If the method of baptizing is unimportant, as is claimed by many denominations, then we ought to see good evidence of that in early historical accounts of varying practice by the churches. If sprinkling is more correct, then there certainly should be evidence of theological clarification by the early church leaders. Did you know that the Greek Orthodox church still immerses its babies? There must be some reason for that. If, on the other hand, the Bible teaches immersion of believers as an exclusive ordinance, then history ought to show that such was the case until some big changes took place in the doctrinal soundness of the churches.

The second area we need to look at relates to the question of when the churches started to baptize babies. Did you know that many of the churches that sprinkle their babies do not try to justify their practice from Scripture, but rather point to the length of time that other churches have done it? If that is true, then history should provide adequate proof that such was the case from the earliest days of the church. If, on the other hand, the Bible will not allow for the inclusion of infant children in the ordinance of baptism, then, surely, history would show that the churches resisted the incorrect practices and were diligent in their efforts to discipline and restore erring assemblies. History should help us know what was taught and practiced by those who were closest to the Lord's own teaching. We won't be able to "prove" anything by that, but we surely should have a better idea of what happened than we do now.

However, as valuable as a knowledge of history can be for us, it can't hold a candle to the words of Scripture. Since God inspired the Bible, then every word of the Bible is vital for us to understand; and this holds true for the words of Scripture related to baptism. An examination of these words in context should develop evidence that will clearly support one mode of baptism, or supply evidence that any mode is permissible. Surely, the Holy Spirit would not leave us up in the air about something that important.

A word of caution is in order here. Often a student becomes so caught up with the research of the historical stories, or so involved with the technicalities of the linguistic scholars, that he forgets to search the only source of absolute truth available. One danger that you must avoid in a study of the Scriptures, however, is the temptation to check the opinions and "interpretations" of your favorite Bible scholar before you research the words of Scripture. These commentators give invaluable assistance to the serious Bible student, but they are only men. Men can, and do, filter their study through preconceived ideas. The only way for you to avoid such filtering is to look at every passage of Scripture that could possibly relate to the doctrine you are studying. This will enable you to carefully construct from Scripture alone the teaching that is warranted. If, and when, a Bible commentator augments the study through insight given to him by the Holy Spirit, then you are able to grasp that insight more readily. If, however, a commentator has incorrectly applied, or inadvertantly ignored a portion of the information within the Scriptures, then you are able to recognize the incorrect or missing information at once. For those reasons, this book will do just that. We will look at those passages in the Bible that relate to the ordinance of baptism, and we will see what the Bible teaches.

Do you remember the promise in Deuteronomy 29:29? "The secret things belong unto the Lord our God: but those things which are revealed belong unto us and to our children forever, that we may do all the words of this law." God has made a special effort to reveal everything that is necessary for us to know. His creation reveals "the invisible things" of God, "even his eternal power and Godhead" (Romans 1:20). Do you remember that the Apostle Peter specified that "his divine power hath given unto us all things that pertain unto life and godliness . . ." (II Peter 1:3)? It seems as though God has provided enough information in the world, in the history of His people, and in His Word to satisfy even the most hard-to-convince person around. Maybe one point or one piece of evidence is not enough for a genuine skeptic, but when all the evidence has been examined, there should be enough data to demonstrate the correct mode and practice for the administration of the ordinance of baptism. If there is not enough evidence, or the evidence is not clear, you will be satisfied that you have the perfect right to choose for yourself whatever mode and practice seem most fitting.

Chapter 2

When Did The Differences Start?

You would think that with all the churches that sprinkle, there would be a whole lot of books claiming the early churches practiced sprinkling. But that just isn't so. There are no scholars who maintain that immersion was not a mode of the early churches. Nor are there any who show that immersion is not taught as a mode of baptism by the Scriptures. Of all the great Christian men of the past and present who support either sprinkling or pouring as an acceptable mode of baptism, not one supports his view on Scripture alone. In fact, most of them admit rather candidly that the mode of the Scripture, and the mode of the early churches was immersion.

Surprised?

So was I.

Philip Schaff, a Presbyterian, whose

marvelous *History of the Christian Church* has been the standard source of modern scholarship, admits that immersion was the mode of the New Testament era because of: "The usual form of the original meaning of the Greek *baptidzein* and *baptismos;* from the analogy of John's baptism in the Jordan; from the apostle's comparison of the sacred rite with the miraculous passage of the Red Sea, with the escape of the ark from the flood, with a cleansing and refreshing bath, and with burial and resurrection; finally, from the general custom of the ancient church, which prevails in the East to this day." Even Earle Cairns, who is the head of the history department at Wheaton College and a strong supporter of sprinkling, admits in his book, *Christianity Through the Centuries*: "Immersion seems to have been widely practiced in the first century, but . . ." Cairns hastens to add, "according to the *Didache*, baptism could be performed by pouring water over the head of the one being baptized if no stream of running water or large amount of water were available."

These two examples from well-known and respected church historians are highly representative of the position of most non-immersionist writers. I would not want to bore you by repeating numerous statements of non-immersionist writers from the early centuries through the late nineteenth century. However, it is certainly worth your knowing that all of these writers from the centuries of Christian scholarship declare freely and with one voice that immersion is taught by the Scripture, and that immersion was the common practice of the churches in the early centuries after Christ.

Since this is so, it makes you wonder what happened to cause a change in the practice of immersion. Indeed, when did this take place? How can such a change be justified? Since the Scriptures support the mode of immersion, what do you think happened in the doctrinal discussion of the churches that encouraged a divergence from the common practice of the churches? These questions need answers.

Do you remember the quotation from Earle Cairns? A reference was made to the *Didache* and its support for other modes of baptism. The section of that document that deals with baptism makes this statement: "Now concerning baptism, thus baptize ye: having first uttered all these things, baptize into the name of the Father, and of the Holy Spirit, in running water. But if thou hast not running water, baptize in other water; and if thou canst not in cold, then in warm. But if thou hast neither, pour water upon the head thrice, into the name of the Father, and Son, and Holy Spirit. But before the baptism let the baptizer and the baptized fast, and whatsoever others can; but the baptized thou shalt command to fast for two or three days before." Obviously, this instruction allows for an alternative mode for baptism if immersion cannot be performed. But, we need to know the origin and the date of this document since it is important as an evidence of the earlier churches.

There is no clear agreement among historians about the *Didache*. It is properly called

"The Teaching of the Twelve Apostles" and is variously dated from as early as A.D. 130, all the way through the fourth century. Philip Schaff, in his *History of the Christian Church*, speaks for the majority of conservative historians in his discussion of the *Didache*. He concludes that it "is the oldest and simplest church manual, of Jewish Christian (Palestinian or Syrian) origin, from the end of the first century, known to the Greek fathers, but only recently discovered and published by Bryennios (1883)."

The substance of the *Didache* was known primarily through the seventh book of *The Apostolic Constitutions*, a lengthy church manual which was brought into its present form by unknown authors from early oral traditions and creedal forms. The first six books were composed at the end of the third century, in Syria, and seem to have been compiled through the work of the Eastern Church in an effort to establish the episcopal theocracy. These *Constitutions*, along with the expanded *Didache*, never did become accepted as formal authority, and, according to Schaff, were rejected for heretical interpolations by the Trullan Council of A.D. 692.

I give you all this information only to demonstrate the questions that exist about the information contained in the *Didache*. Those scholars who want to find evidence for sprinkling are generally positive in their treatment of the accuracy and historicity of the *Didache*. Those scholars who favor immersion tend to be less charitable toward it. However, whatever may be the case as to date and origin, the *Didache* does give concrete evidence that there were baptismal changes taking place as far back as the beginning of the second century. Still, it is clear from this document that immersion was the preferred form.

The first real evidence of an instance of baptism by a mode other than immersion was that of Novatian, the founder of an anti-Catholic sect that flourished in the middle of the third century. Evidently, while Novatian was still being instructed in the catechism necessary for baptism in the custom of that day, "he was supposed to lie at the point of death, and asked baptism in order to save his soul, but could not be three times immersed, as was the practice. Yet, something must be done, and that in a hurry; so, while stretched on his bed, water was poured all round his person, in an outline inclosing his whole body; then, it was poured all over him till he was drenched, making perfusion as near an immersion as possible" (from Thomas Armitage's *History of the Baptists*). This effort was understood, evidently, by the church authorities of that day to be sufficient to "save" Novatian in case of his death, but was not considered good enough to act as "regular" baptism were Novatian to regain his health.

One of the earliest historians to examine that period of time was Eusebius, who lived scarcely a hundred years after the events surrounding Novatian. In *Ecclesiastical History*, he records the answer of Novatian's bishop to a letter written to him about Novatian's "baptism": ". . . when attached with an obstinate disease, and being supposed at the point of death, was baptized by aspersion, in the bed on which he lay; if, indeed, it be proper to say that one like him did receive baptism." Obviously, the mode of baptism was not considered satisfactory by the majority church leadership of that time. In fact, that was one of the reasons that the Roman Church later came to reject the Novatians as heretics.

Cyprian, who was the Bishop of Carthage during the time of Novatian, defended the use of aspersion for immersion on the basis that "the sprinkling of water prevails equally with the washing of salvation; and that when this is done in the church, when the faith both of the receiver and giver is sound, all things hold and may be consummated and perfected by the majesty of the Lord, and by the truth of faith" (from *A Short History of the Baptists*). However, it was a long time before this view became accepted by the general church. There did not seem to be disagreement among the Roman Church as to the saving effect of a little water, but it was felt that this so-called "clinic" baptism was an unsatisfactory form. Ordination was refused to those who had been "clinically" baptized for a long time after Novatian, simply because the widely accepted mode was immersion. Those who deviated from immersion, even though there were the most distressing of circumstances, were not considered to have had "real" baptism.

If you have been reading "between the lines," you have noticed that these men who supported sprinkling seemed to have other doctrinal problems as well. We'll go into those problems in more detail in the next chapter, but you should be aware that the churches of the second and third centuries were in a real mess! Let me reconstruct the scene.

All of the apostles had died by the end of the first century. The New Testament had been written, but was not collected into the complete form until sometime in the fourth century. Most of the churches circulated the handwritten copies of the various letters and Gospels among themselves. And, as visitors from other churches would bring copies of other letters from one of the apostles, the letters would be copied and kept in the church library. There were a lot of fake letters around, too. In fact, the Apostle Paul warned the church at Thessalonica that they were not to be shaken up by false teaching about the Lord's return, "Neither by spirit, nor by word, nor by letter as from us . . ." (II Thessalonians 2:2). In other words, there were forgers and false religionists even in Paul's day!

But, the beauty of the Lord's church structure was that it was not controlled by one man . . . or at least wasn't at the start. Those many churches, scattered all over the civilized world, began to do what the Berean Christians had done: they "searched the Scriptures daily, whether those things were so" (Acts 17:11). Nearly all of the churches had copies of the complete Old Testament. The Septuagint, a Greek translation of the Old Testament, was in common use by the time the Lord Jesus came.

All of the apostles used the Septuagint as their "Bible" when they went out to establish other churches, and the people of those churches were used to studying in the Old Testament to see "whether those things were so." So, when a fake "Epistle" would surface, or "another gospel" (Galatians 1:6) would be found, the churches would check them out against the Old Testament and the teachings of those letters they knew to be genuine. If they didn't measure up, they were destroyed.

However, there were groups of people who were not really interested in following the "apostles' doctrine." As a matter of fact, when the Apostle John wrote his first letter around the close of the first century, there were some people who had left the churches to form their own "denomination." He says: "They went out from us, but they were not of us; for if they had been of us, they would no doubt have continued with us: but they went out, that they might be made manifest that were not all of us" (I John 2:19). These people who "went out" began to form the bad seeds that would later grow into the false church system of the Roman Catholic Church. Satan doesn't waste much time in counterfeiting God's work. He always tries to "deceive the very elect" (Matthew 24:24).

With all that mess going on when the apostles were alive, it's no wonder that things were worse by the third century. The wonder is that the churches were able to keep as pure as they did. Unfortunately, it is the nature of people to write about sensational things. The ordinary, everyday humdrum of living doesn't make for stimulating reading, so we tend to write letters and compose books about the unordinary. Well, the writers of the early centuries were no different. They wrote back and forth to each other about the "problems" and tried to refute or defend some "unusual" idea. That's okay, but it leaves us with a rather distorted view of the magnitude of the "problems."

When we go back into the writings of these early centuries, almost everything deals with some departure from the apostles' teaching. There were, however, hundreds of churches and thousands of people in nearly every country of the civilized world who were not involved in these controversies. They didn't write any letters or books, because they didn't need to. Their church fellowships were doing well! The letters and books were written in those areas, mostly in the big cities, where there were "hot" issues being debated. One of those issues was baptism.

We've looked at a few of the men who were trying to change the method of baptism from immersion to sprinkling. They based their arguments mainly on the wrong teaching that baptism was necessary for salvation, and that a little water was just as good as a whole lot. To get a fair comparison, you ought to look at a few men who, although still believing that baptism was necessary to save, did not believe that sprinkling was good enough. They based their argument on the teaching of the Scriptures and the apostles. One such man was

Hermes, who may have been addressed by the Apostle Paul in Romans 16:14. In *A Concise History of Baptists* G. H. Orchard reports that Hermes had this to say about baptism around A.D. 95: "Before a man receives the name of the Son of God, he is ordained to death; but when he receives that seal, he is freed from death, and delivered unto life: now that seal is water, into which men descend under an obligation to death, but ascend out of it, being appointed unto life."

And, according to the same book, Irenaeus, pastor of a church at Lyons around A.D. 180, wrote a rather stern note regretting the conduct of some "who thought it needless to bring the person to the water at all; but mixing oil and water together, they pour it on the candidate's head."

Tertullian, whose writings had a wide effect on Roman church development and theology during the early centuries, had this to say in his tract *De Baptismo*, chapter 12: "Others make the suggestion that the apostles then served the turn of baptism when in their little ship they were sprinkled and covered with the waves; that Peter himself also was immersed enough when he walked on the sea. It is, however, as I think, one thing to be sprinkled or intercepted by the violence of the sea; and another to be baptized in obedience to the discipline of religion" (from Strong's *Systematic Theology*). In chapter 4 of that same tract, according to G. H. Orchard, Tertullian answers the question that some were having concerning the proper place of baptism. "It is all one whether a person is washed in the sea or in a pond, in a fountain or in a river, in standing or in running water; nor is there any difference between those whom John baptized in Jordan, and those whom Peter baptized, unless it be supposed that the eunuch whom Philip dipped in the water, obtained more or less salvation." This response by Tertullian may well have been generated by the so-called "Teaching of the Twelve Apostles" that we looked at earlier.

All of this evidence seems to lead to the conclusion that a change in the method of baptism was being formulated as early as the middle of the second century. If the *Didache* is accurately dated at A.D. 130-220, and if these rebuttals by Tertullian and Irenaeus are correctly transmitted to us, we are justified in observing a trend toward sprinkling as early as A.D. 130-160. You should be careful to note, however, that the majority of Christians were not in favor of the modal change, and, in fact, were harshly denouncing it. The churches in the areas where the Novatians were strong refused to accept the immersion of the Novatian sect, simply because their leader had not been properly baptized. There were many churches of these first three centuries that were not allied with the emerging system of the Roman church, and all of these were strongly supporting the Biblical teaching of immersion. These non-allied churches were in the habit of rebaptizing any who came to their membership because they were unsure of the purity of the doctrines of the allied churches. All of these many writings and practices of several different "denominations" tell us that immersion was the majority practice at least through the first three hundred years after the Lord Jesus Christ founded His church. That is worth knowing. The churches that practice sprinkling today have to explain why there was so much resistance to sprinkling . . . if sprinkling is all right.

Chapter 3

What Caused
The Changes?

Perhaps the first error that began to develop toward the end of the first century was the concept of a clerical hierarchy among the leaders of the churches. That is, some of the church pastors decided they were more important than some others, and began to boss things. The Apostle John writes in his third epistle about "Diotrophes, who loveth to have the preeminence among them, receiveth us not. Wherefore, if I come, I will remember his deeds which he doeth, prating against us with malicious words: and not content therewith, neither doth he himself receive the brethren, and forbiddeth them that would, and casteth them out of the church" (III John 9,10). This terrible error was paving the way for many abuses in the years to come.

The Lord had specifically told His apostles

that they were not to set up any kind of boss-worker relationship in His church. In Matthew 20:25-28, He announced: "Ye know that the princes of the Gentiles exercise dominion over them, and they that are great exercise authority upon them. But it shall not be so among you: but whosoever will be great among you, let him be your minister; And whosoever will be chief among you, let him be your servant: Even as the Son of man came not to be ministered unto, but to minister, and to give his life a ransom for many."

There is a whole lot of information packed into those three little verses. The Lord asked the apostles to observe how the "princes" of the Gentiles "exercise dominion," and how the "great" persons "exercise authority." The word for "prince" is a general word that was used for the person who had the first political rank in the area. He could be a judge or an area chief. The term just meant "top dog." The "great" person was somebody important. The word means "big." These two kinds of "muck-ity-mucks" are present in every society. They "wheel and deal" and "exercise dominion" and "authority" over anybody they can!

The word translated "exercise authority" is used only in Matthew. It means "to have full privilege, to be first in pleasure." The word translated "exercise dominion" is used only two other times in the New Testament. It means "to subjugate, to control." Once, when the Apostle Paul was preaching in Corinth, some holier-than-thou Jews thought they would get in on the religion bandwagon by trying their hand at casting out demons. When they pompously commanded the demons to go away, the demons answered back, "Jesus I know, and Paul I know; but who are ye? And the man in whom the evil spirit was leaped on them, and overcame them, and prevailed against them, so that they fled out of that house naked and wounded" (Acts 19:15,16). The word "overcame" is the same word as "exercise dominion" in Matthew 20. You can see how strongly distasteful this word is.

The other time this word is used, it is right in the middle of one of the clearest teachings in the Bible about the job of the pastor. Peter was wrapping up his first letter with some summary commands to the various churches. He says in I Peter 5:1-3: "The elders which are among you I exhort, who am also an elder . . . Feed the flock of God which is among you, taking the oversight thereof, not by constraint, but willingly; not for filthy lucre, but of a ready mind; Neither as being lords over God's heritage, but being ensamples to the flock." I don't know how it could have been made much plainer. If you want to be in charge of God's flock, you are to be an example—not a boss. The words "being lords over" are the translation of the same word used by the Lord in Matthew 20, and by Luke in Acts 19.

But it wasn't long before bossism lifted its ugly head in the church in full disregard of these clear warnings of Scripture. Some of the more capable preachers became important enough to be the "advisors" of other men, then they were given responsibility for the larger churches from which they tended to "oversee" the operations and doctrine of smaller cities. The "pastor" was relegated to serve in charge of only one church, and usually that was a small one. The term "priest" was substituted for "pastor" sometime in the second century. The "bishop" was distinguished from the "pastor" mainly by the size of the church at first, but later became synonymous with an "overseer" in charge of an area with other churches under him. These developments did not take place all at once, nor were they prevalent in every area at the same time. Rather, they found strength in first one place, then another, until by the middle of the third century, the practice of a church hierarchy was fairly well established.

Thomas Armitage, whose tremendous work on *The History of the Baptists* has never been equaled, has this to say about a man named Cyprian: "Thus, by the close of the third century we have ... an episcopacy with which is lodged eternal life, a 'Catholic Church,' outside of which are all heretics, and no salvation out of the church. For this, Cyprian, a converted pagan, Naetorician and bishop of Carthage, is more to blame than any other man...." Evidently, Cyprian was a real force in uniting the erring churches into an organized unit behind the power of the episcopacy. According to Armitage, Cyprian once wrote an answer to a man named Pupianus, who was questioning the authority of the church leaders in the matters of changing Biblical teaching: "What presumption! What arrogance! What pride it is, to call the prelates and priests to account! The bees have their queen; the armies have their generals; and they preserve their loyalty; the robbers obey their captains with humble obsequiousness! How much more upright, and how much better are the unreasonable and dumb animals, and bloody robbers, and swords and weapons, than you are. There the rule is acknowledged and feared, whom not a divine mandate has set up, but whom the reprobate souls have appointed of themselves." Cyprian goes on to berate this poor man and denounce him as a "fool," warn him of "hell-fire," and castigate his froward presumption against the priests.

This position generated a usurpation of the authority of the Scriptures by a few men who were privileged to control the authority of the church. Cairns writes in *Christianity Through the Centuries*, "Emphasis upon the monarchal bishop who, it was believed, derived his authority by apostolic succession, led many to think of him as a center of unity. The depository of truth and the dispenser of the means of the grace of God through the sacraments."

For some time prior to Cyprian, the churches had begun extensive training and initiation of their leaders. A subculture of "priests" began to grow within the confines of the training sessions that led some of these men to start "denominations" of their own, as Novatian did. Others were content to identify with the growing movement that considered Rome as the major church. Still others were isolating themselves into small pockets of churches and would have nothing to do with anyone else. These various movements gave the momentum to other doctrinal errors that otherwise might have been squelched by the membership of the churches themselves. Since the membership had grown to tolerate leaders who were authoritarian rather than exemplary, they had relinquished the responsibility that the Apostle Paul said was more noble "in that they searched the scriptures daily to see whether these things were so" (Acts 17:11).

All the while that church hierarchy was developing another more influential doctrinal error began to rise. It was the concept of baptismal regeneration. No one is able to provide any concrete reasoning for its rise, but it does seem likely that the very importance of the ordinance was the main factor. Bible commentators of the centuries have said that the act of baptism is not merely an optional rite of religious significance, but that it must be observed by those who would be obedient to the commandment of the Lord. The Lord Himself walked some sixty miles to submit Himself to this ordinance in order to "fulfil all righteousness" (Matthew 3:15). The apostles continued to baptize during the Lord's ministry on earth, and then were commanded to baptize all the disciples that were to be made throughout the entire age (Matthew 28:19).

With that much emphasis in the Scriptures, it's not hard to see why some preachers would speak long and hard about the necessity of such obedience, and eventually come to think of the ordinance as more than symbolism.

Then, too, many areas of the world were very hard on the Christian. Perhaps it was thought that an emphasis on the necessity of baptism would motivate some to salvation. Or, perhaps, that the act was a special means of securing God's favor and protection against persecution. Whatever may have been the thinking, the emphasis on the necessity soon turned to teaching that it was a requirement for salvation.

The progress of this doctrine during these early years is fairly easy to see in the writings of the church leaders. Do you remember the early creed, "The Teaching of the Twelve Apostles"? In the section dealing with baptism, the authors required fasting before the ordinance could take place. This was an addition to the Scriptural teaching, probably because they wanted the candidate to be "sure" of his commitment to the Lord.

By the time of Justin Martyr, a proselyte to the Jewish religion who embraced Christianity about A.D. 150, this idea of saving power in the waters had gained prominence. G. H. Orchard quotes Justin: "As many as are persuaded and believe that these things which are taught by us are true, and do promise to live according to them, are directed first to pray, and ask God, with fasting, the forgiveness of their sins: and we also pray and fast together with them. Then we bring them to some place where there is water; and they are regenerated by the same way of regeneration by which we are regenerated: for they are washed in the name of the Father. . . ."

The events that solidified the error of baptismal regeneration into established teaching were various church creeds formed under the direction of church councils. One of the first major councils was held in Nicea. The early churches came with a mind ready to find some unifying structures among themselves. They were "battle-weary" from all the dissension, and had tacitly agreed among themselves to follow the outcome of the council. This, of course, would not have been the case were it not for the power taken by the "bishops" away from the churches themselves. This council took place in A.D. 325 and produced the Nicene Creed. That creed was a fairly sound statement of basic theology, which was modified some by the various churches, and eventually came to have this statement in it about baptism: "I acknowledge one Baptism for the remission of sins. . . ." When you compare this Nicene Creed with the Apostles' Creed written some years earlier, it is easy to see the addition of the phrase concerning baptism. The other points are virtually identical.

About fifty years later, in A.D. 381 the churches held another council in Constantinople in an effort to dogmatize much of the eroding faith of the new state religion. The theological work of that council was summarized in a Synodical Letter written in 382. It had this to say about baptism: "This is the faith that ought to be sufficient for you, for us, for all who wrest not the word of the true faith; for it is the ancient faith; it is the faith of our baptism; it is the faith that teaches us to believe in the name of the Father, of the Son, and of the Holy Ghost" (from *The Translations of Social Order* by Rousas J. Rushdoony).

You will observe that these creeds, while based on a lengthy discussion by many "bishops" on the things of the Scriptures, do not in and of themselves quote or praise the Scriptures. This subtle drift from the authority of the Word of God to the "word of the true faith" is the major common denominator of all error. The church councils *discussed* the Word, *philosophized* about the Word, *argued* about the Word, and finally *substituted* their words about the Word for the Word itself. The result was devastating!

Chapter 4

What About Infant Baptism?

One of the most unusual discoveries in church history is the fact that sprinkling and babies were not connected. If you are like most persons, you really don't separate the two ideas, because every church that sprinkles today sprinkles babies. Oh, they will sprinkle adults if asked, but sprinkling is most often associated with infants. But, did you know that the Eastern Orthodox church (sometimes known as the Greek Orthodox) immerses its infants? In fact, the issue of sprinkling versus immersion was one of the factors that caused the Eastern Church system to split off from the Roman system in A.D. 1054. There was no disagreement among the Roman and Greek clerics about the age of the subject to be baptized, only as to the mode.

Up until now our research has been centered

around the modal change that took place gradually through the first three centuries. There are many other authors who have taken great pains to demonstrate that immersion was the majority practice until well into the fifth century among the Western churches. It really isn't necessary to go over all that information with you since we aren't trying to debate the length of time involved. However, you should be aware that many historians document the practice of immersion much further than others. We do need to know, however, what happened between the later third century and the middle eleventh century that allowed the inclusion of infant children into the ordinance of baptism.

Every church historian agrees that the practice of infant baptism was unknown to the age of the apostles. In his *History of the Christian Church*, Schaff says, "The apostolic origin of infant baptism is denied not only by the Baptist, but also by many paedobaptist divines. ... It is true, the apostolic church was a missionary church, and had first to establish a mother community, in the bosom of which alone the grace of baptism can be improved by Christian education. ... True, the New Testament contains no express command to baptize infants; such a command would not agree with the free spirit of the gospel. Nor was there any compulsory or general infant baptism before the union of church and state." That lengthy quotation is representative of hundreds of such admissions from churchmen and scholars who now practice the sprinkling of infants. Their support for such practice must come from a later date and another source than the Scriptures and the practice of the Apostolic Age.

You know what? That's a real problem. If it is all right to "invent" or "improve" something in the Scriptures, then it seems as though it would be all right to do whatever you please. We have already seen how the various church councils began to produce "creeds" that superceded the Scriptures in authority. Why, that's no different from the Mormons, the Jehovah's Witnesses, the Christian Scientists, or a whole host of other cults who base their "religion" on the revelations of men which they consider to be superior to the Scriptures. These early churches evidently forgot or ignored the warning of the Lord Jesus in Matthew 5:19: "Whosoever therefore shall break one of these least commandments, and shall teach men so, he shall be called the least in the kingdom of heaven: but whosoever shall do and teach them, the same shall be called great in the kingdom of heaven." The churches that sprinkle babies today must provide an answer to this obvious change from the practice of the New Testament.

The earliest clear evidence for the existence of infant baptism is the rebuke by Tertullian opposing the practice in A.D. 185. The first writer who was in favor of such a change in the subjects of baptism was the Carthaginian bishop, Cyprian. In a rather large synod meeting that he called together in A.D. 253, the sixty-four bishops under his lead debated the delay recommended by Tertullian in giving baptism. Both Tertullian and Cyprian strongly believed in baptismal regeneration, but Tertullian felt that it was impossible for mortal sins to be forgiven by the church after baptism. The question for this synod in Carthage was not whether children should be baptized, but whether they should be baptized as early as the second or third day. The overall result was a compromise to allow the early baptism of infants at the option of the parents or priest, and still practice the baptism of older persons.

Keep in mind that although the mode of baptism was being changed during this same period, the majority of churches were still immersing adults. As a matter of fact, the early councils of the church were against infant baptism. The Council of Elvira or Grenada in A.D. 305 required the delay of baptism for two years. The Council of Laodicea held in A.D. 360 demanded that those who were "to be baptized must learn the creed by heart and recite it." A major council held in Constantinople in A.D. 368 made the decree that persons desiring baptism should "remain a long time under Scriptural instruction before they receive baptism." And the Council of Carthage which met in 398 declared that "catechumens shall give their names, and be prepared for baptism." Even though the Roman Catholic church system was becoming well formed and very powerful, there were many churches that still refused to follow the lead of those who were promoting variance from the Scriptural principles.

Surely the most influential writer of this period was Augustine, the bishop of Hippo-Regius in North Africa. He lived from A.D. 353-430. Even though Augustine was not himself baptized in infancy, he strongly defended such practice. His writings were responsible for a rash of encyclical statements (those things are official letters from the church "headquarters") being formed and delivered to the churches by several different councils. The Council of Mela, in Numidia, A.D. 416, was called and led by Augustine. In his *A History of the Baptists*, John T. Christian reports that these fifteen persons decreed: "Also it is the pleasure of the bishops in order that whoever denies that infants newly born of their mothers, are to be baptized or says that baptism is administered for the remission of their own sins, but not an account of original sin, delivered from Adam, and to be expiated by the laver of regeneration, be accursed."

In another council held in Carthage in A.D. 418, over two hundred bishops from all over Africa issued a list of eight Canons (the "Canon" was a rule of the church) which bore the easily identifiable mark of Augustine. This council had been called to deal with the rising popularity of the teachings of Pelagius, a British monk, who was teaching that unbaptized children were saved. The main tone of the second Canon of this council, according to Schaff, was that "Whoever rejects infant baptism, or denies original sin in children, so that the baptismal formula, 'for the remission of sins,' would have to be taken not in a strict, but in a loose sense, let him be anathema." This same council had to deal with the concept of infant salvation prior to baptism, and said, "Whoever says, that in the kingdom of heaven, or elsewhere, there is a certain middle place, where children dying without baptism live happy, while yet without baptism they cannot enter into the kingdom of heaven, i.e., into eternal life, let him be anathema."

It is fairly easy to see that the doctrine of baptismal regeneration is the main thesis of these rulings on infant baptism. These men were reasoning that it would be foolish, and even wrong, to forbid the baptism of infant children since the baptismal waters were necessary to wash away sins. In fact, it would be unthinkable for someone to delay baptism when the means of salvation was so readily available. Furthermore, it would be so much better to secure salvation for a child before it had the chance to become hardened by a sinful life, and perhaps not submit to baptism at all.

After these councils of the late fourth and fifth centuries, the unity of the Roman Catholic system began to solidify. They already had the backing of the Roman Empire, and were strongly in place in Africa, Spain, England and the Middle East. Churches that differed with the Roman Encyclical Letters or Canons were beginning to fade into a minority as far as their influence was concerned. Most of those churches were in the smaller, more remote areas of the countries, and were not able to avail themselves of the councils or political contact that the larger city churches had. For the most part, they rejected the church-state association, the unscriptural authority of the major city-bishops, and the baptism of infants.

During this time, most of the churches, both those going into the Roman system and others, were not involved in as much controversy over the mode as they were over the subjects. Schaff notes that "notwithstanding this general admission of infant baptism, the practice of it was by no means universal. Forced baptism, which is contrary to the nature of Christianity and the sacrament, was as yet unknown."

There were, at the time, a large number of people who refused to be baptized, mainly because they were afraid that they might sin again and not have the opportunity to be cleansed. John T. Christian indicates that Basil the Great, who became a bishop of Caesarea and metropolitan of all Cappadocia in A.D. 370, wrote a rather remarkable rebuke of this unsound practice some ten years later. "Do you demur and loiter and put off baptism? When you have been from a child catechized in the Word, and you are not yet acquainted with the truth? Having been always learning it, are you not yet come to the knowledge of it? A seeker all your life long. A considerer till you are old. When will you make a Christian? When shall we see you as one of us? Last year you were staying till this year; and now you have a mind to stay till next year. Take heed, that by promising yourself a longer life, you do not quite miss of your hope." Basil believed in baptismal regeneration, and he may well have supported infant baptism, but he does note that the practice was not at all the common affair in his day.

The first rule that is recorded favoring infant baptism in Europe was made by the Spanish Council of Gerunda, A.D. 517. This council was composed of seven bishops who developed ten rules of practice for the churches under their charge. The rule covering the doctrine of infant baptism was made in Article V: "But concerning little sons lately born, it pleaseth us to appoint, that if, as is usual, they be infirm, and do not suck their mother's milk, even on the same day in which they are born, if they be offered, if they be brought, they may be baptized." There is no provision made here for healthy infants, since the dominant practice was still to teach the children preceding baptism. However, since the doctrine of baptismal regeneration was held so strongly, these men felt it "unchristian" to leave a child that was near death unbaptized and out of Heaven.

It is hard for the modern church member to distinguish between the practice of infant baptism and sprinkling since all Western churches that perform baptism on infants do so by sprinkling. Although the sprinkling of infants was virtually unknown until the late sixth century, the immersion of infants was practiced more freely. There are six elaborate descriptions or rituals of baptism that have been preserved for us from these first 600 years. Initially, the so-called *Egyptian Acts* and the *Canon Hipolyte* of the early third century gave a format for church liturgy. Later, Cyril of Jerusalem in A.D. 286 outlined a rather lengthy ritual to follow in baptism. Then the *Apostolic Constitutions* were written around A.D.

350-400 giving more instructions, followed by orders from Ambrose of Milan in A.D. 397, and Dionysius Areopagita in A.D. 450. Each of these "Acts" became well known in the Roman churches and every one of them advocated immersion.

Well, we still have the question, At what time did the majority of Christianity practice infant baptism? This question is almost impossible to answer clearly. Part of the problem lies in the scarcity of documents dealing with the non-Roman churches, and part of the problem lies in the dilemma of accepting much of the Roman system as "Christian." Most historians concede that the papal system became fairly corrupt around the sixth century, and continued in despicable conditions through the Reformation. There were many godly men in the monasteries, and there is evidence that many of the individual priests of isolated areas were sincere believers. However, the bulk of the churches were so corrupt that the common man lived in fear of the clergy. It has been estimated by J. M. Carroll in *The Trail of Blood* that some fifty million persons were killed by the Roman Catholic hierarchy between the fifth and sixteenth centuries. Obviously, if that many were killed, a significant number of "other" churches were not accepting the doctrine and practice of the Roman system.

If you accept the Roman churches as the "true" line of Christian church growth, it would be safe to say that a majority of churches practiced infant baptism by the middle of the seventh century, certainly by the eighth.

However, it is the contention of many sincere Christian scholars that the Roman system was so corrupted by its error and carnality that it became an empty shell, consisting of great political and financial power, but devoid of the presence of the Holy Spirit. If you hold to that position, then it is safe to say that infant baptism did not become a majority practice until well after the Reformation.

Well, what do we have so far? History is a good teacher, but the lesson is fairly difficult to dig out. Back in chapter two, we found out that the churches didn't start sprinkling until the second century, and that it didn't become anywhere near a majority practice until the sixth or seventh century. In chapter three we saw that the changes were started by two terrible heresies: the practice of a church hierarchy, and the teaching that baptism will save you. Those two errors were the core of many other changes, but were the main basis for the start of infant baptism in the third century. This chapter has traced the development of that change from its very meager start until its common practice between the seventh and eighth centuries—at least by the Roman Catholic system.

History has taught us that immersion was the practice of the first churches well into the sixth century, and that adults or knowledgeable children were the main subjects of baptism even beyond that. Obviously, the churches that practice the sprinkling of babies cannot depend on history to provide any real help.

Chapter 5

Does Language Allow Sprinkling?

These next few chapters are going to demand a little more patience and concentration from you than before. You may not have any training in the Biblical languages, but—and this is a big *but*—there isn't any shortcut to a thorough examination of the words of Scripture without looking at the Greek and Hebrew, the languages God used to record His infallible Word. Now, take heart—you don't have to have formal training to check the languages; there are a lot of study books on the market that can help you get the information.

Perhaps it would be good to explain to you what we are going to do. Anytime we need to study out a broad teaching in Scripture, we have to start with the English words that might express that teaching. In this case, we want to find out if "baptism" can be administered by any method. So, we would check words like "sprinkle," "wash," "pour," "bathe," as well as "baptize." In our check of these words, we would first have to go to an exhaustive concordance to find out what Greek or Hebrew word is involved.

Since we are dealing with the New Testament for the most part, we will mainly be concerned with Greek words. Each English word may well have two or more Greek words that are close enough to be translated by the same English term, but have a distinctive meaning. We have to know what those Greek words are, and then we have to find out their basic meaning. We can do that through the language dictionary of a good concordance, like the *Stong's Exhaustive Concordance*, or we can go to any number of excellent language lexicons. Once we know the basic definition, we have to check every reference in Scripture where that word is used to see if it has anything to do with the ordinance of baptism. If it does, we can use that word and its appropriate definition to help us understand how to baptize.

Did you follow all that? Well if you didn't, don't worry too much; it will become much more clear as we get into the study itself.

There are two words which are used by the New Testament writers to describe the action of sprinkling. One of these words appears only once in the entire Bible. It is the Greek word, *proschusis*, and is found in Hebrews 11:28 where the writer is discussing the faith that Moses demonstrated in keeping the passover by "sprinkling" the blood of the passover lamb on the doorposts of the houses. The word carries the idea of pouring, and is an excellent word to describe the action taken by the children of Israel when they were told to "strike it [the blood] on the two side posts and on the upper door posts of the houses" (Exodus 12:7).

The other word is *rantidzo*. This word is found four times as a verb and twice as a noun in the New Testament, and some eight times in the Greek translation of the Old Testament. The verses in the New Testament (Hebrews 9:13,19,21; 10:22; 12:24; I Peter 1:2) describe the sprinkling action. Each of them deals with the relationship that the blood sacrifice of the Lord Jesus had to the pictures drawn by the sacrifices of the Old Testament law.

One verse that is of particular importance to the study of the baptismal ordinance is Hebrews 10:22. That verse says: "Let us draw near with a true heart in full assurance of faith, having our hearts sprinkled [*rantidzo*] from an evil conscience, and our bodies washed with pure water." Many of the early writers used this verse to justify the necessity of baptism for salvation. And, since the word for sprinkle was used in parallel with the word for wash, they said that the mode was immaterial. However, that reference is to the fulfillment of the sacrificial work of the Lord Jesus, not to the ordinance of baptism.

It is possible that the second part of Hebrews 10:22, "our bodies washed with pure water," may have reference to the ordinance of baptism, but whatever may be the significance of that possibility, it bears no theological relationship to the use of *rantidzo* in the first part. Hebrews 9 has three usages of *rantidzo*, all of which describe the action of the Old Testament priest in his portrayal of Christ's ultimate sacrifice. Peter's use of *rantidzo* is an additional verification of the imagery of Christ's work. He says that we are "elect according to the foreknowledge of God the Father, through sanctification of the Spirit, unto obedience and sprinkling of the blood of Jesus Christ." The Scriptures are consistent; the words for "sprinkle" mean only "sprinkle" and are not used in connection with the ordinance of baptism.

The New Testament uses four different Greek words to describe the various shades of the English word "pour." The most common word is *ekcheo* which is used some eighteen times, and is translated by the English words "pour out," "shed," "shed forth," "spill," and "run out." *Ekcheo* was used by the major classic Greek writers to describe libations to the gods, the "pouring out" of wine or oil or blood to the gods for appeasement. The Old Testament Septuagint uses *ekcheo* in I Samuel 7:6 when it observes that Israel "gathered together to Mizpeh, and drew water, and poured it out before the Lord."

And the marvelous promise of the coming of the Holy Spirit given in Joel 2:28 is very important. God says, "I will pour out my spirit upon all flesh. . . ." When that was fulfilled on the day of Pentecost, the New Testament writer referred to the believers as being "baptized" with the Holy Spirit. Some have tried to show by this connection that pouring is a satisfactory mode of baptism. However, the transfer is not at all warranted. The action described by Joel was the action God would do *with* the Holy Spirit *to* men. The New Testament writers described the effect the action taken *by* God had *upon* men. Luke notes in his record of that event in Acts 2:2 that the house where they were sitting was "filled" and that each person was completely engulfed by the Spirit of God in that room. Later, when Peter spoke of the phenomenon (verses 14-17), he pointed out that the unusual "signs" were a result of the "pouring" (*ekcheo*) of God's Spirit out on everyone. As God "poured" out His Spirit, the people in the house were "filled" with His Spirit, and began to demonstrate great power. There is no justification for relating pouring to immersion in this passage, especially since the ordinance of baptism is not indicated.

You can see the complete distinction of *ekcheo* from any idea of immersion when you study the references where the word is found. In each verse where the English word "pour" is used (Acts 2:17,18; Revelation 16:1-4,8,10, 12,17) the description is either of the Pentecostal outpouring or of the ultimate outpouring of the wrath of God. In every passage where the English word "shed" is used (Acts 2:33; 22:20; Romans 3:15; Titus 3:6; Revelation 16:6) the word describes the pouring out of blood from wounds. And in the remaining references (Matthew 9:17; Mark 2:22; Luke 5:27) the thought is connected with the spilling of wine from bottles. The imagery is perfectly clear. *Ekcheo* means "to pour out; to run out in a stream." The word is never used to describe immersion, nor is it ever used in connection with the ordinance of baptism.

There are two words which are quite similar to *ekcheo*. *Katacheo* is a combination of the word *ekcheo* and the preposition *kata*. Literally, it means "to pour down upon," and is used in Matthew 26:7 and Mark 14:3 where Mary Magdelene broke the precious box of ointment and poured it on Jesus' head. The other of these two similar words is *kerannumi* which can be distinguished in concept merely by the additional idea of mixing some substances together by pouring. It is used in Revelation 14:10 where the Scripture warns that those who bow down to the false Christ will "drink of the wine of the wrath of God, which is poured out without mixture into the cup of his indication." It is also used in Revelation 18:6 where Babylon is told that "the cup which she hath filled [mixed]" will be "mixed" double against her. A good Old Testament example is found in Proverbs 9:5 where the Scripture tells us that wisdom offers a good wine which she has "mingled." Neither of these words is connected in any way with the ordinance of baptism, nor is there any question of the manner of operation. They always mean pour. Not sprinkle. Not immerse.

There is one other word for "pour." It is the Greek word *ballo*, and is found in Matthew 26:12 where the Lord says, "in that she hath poured this ointment on my body, she did it for my burial." It is used again in John 13:5 where the Lord was washing the feet of the disciples. There the Scripture records that He "poured" water into a basin and began to wash their feet. The difference between *ballo* and *ekcheo* is that *ballo* gives the imagery of tossing or casting the liquid rather than gently pouring it. The word is used over a hundred times in the New Testament, most frequently translated by the English word "cast." It is never used in connection with the idea of immersion or with the ordinance of baptism.

Both types of words, the words for "sprinkle" and the words for "pour," always mean exactly what they are supposed to mean. And, that's just what you would expect. The Holy Spirit is not a poor grammarian. He knows how to use language correctly.

Chapter 6

Is Baptism
a Washing?

The words for "wash" or "bathe" are talked about to a great degree by those who try to find a Scriptural basis for some mode of baptism other than immersion. There are six words used by the Holy Spirit to describe the action of washing. Each of these words is unique, but could possibly have been used to convey the idea of the "washing of regeneration" that baptism is supposed to show. *Apolouo* is used only twice in the New Testament, but on both occasions it is possible for the term to be thought of as applying to baptism. The word means "to wash away," or "to wash from."

In I Corinthians 6:11 the apostle reminds the Corinthians that they had been unrighteous sinners, but now "are washed, but ye are sanctified, but ye are justified in the name of the Lord Jesus, and by the Spirit of our God." Some have suggested that the wording here shows a progression of being *washed*, then sanctified, then justified in a similar manner to Romans 8:29,30. If that is so, then "washing" precedes sanctification, and would contradict many passages that teach otherwise. Others suggest that the word may be figurative, but there is clear teaching on sanctification and justification, and it would be highly unlikely that only one word of the three key verbs would be figurative. The word "washed" could refer to the ordinance of baptism, as is sometimes suggested, but that would require baptism before sanctification which is not taught in any of the passages dealing directly with the ordinance. What is clear is that all three of these verbs are performed "by the Spirit of God." This eliminates the ordinance, since it is performed by men. Evidently, the "washed" refers to the action of the Holy Spirit at the time of salvation as is spoken about in Hebrews 9 and 10.

However, this problem is compounded when an examination is made of the usage of *apolouo* in Acts 22:16. There the Apostle Paul is told to "arise, and be baptized, and wash away thy sins, calling on the name of the Lord." This verse seems to demand that a person be baptized to be saved, and is frequently quoted by proponents of such teaching. The linguistics of the sentence are at issue here; the theology of this verse will be discussed later.

The two words "baptize" and "wash away"

are both unusually structured. They are in the middle voice of the Greek verbal structure, which is best translated "baptize yourself" and "wash away yourself." This certainly does not conform to any knowledge, Scriptural or otherwise, about the ordinance of baptism. It would be very difficult to justify this different concept of the ordinance, if that is what it is, with every other reference so diametrically opposed to it. However, it is possible that these words could be translated "Get yourself baptized," and "Get yourself washed away," or that they could be rendered, "Participate in baptism yourself and participate in the washing away of your sins."

This event was recorded as it happened in Acts 9:10-19. According to the instructions given to Ananias from the Lord, he put his hands on Paul and explained: "that thou mightest receive thy sight, and be filled with the Holy Ghost." After the sight was returned, and after he was filled, Paul was baptized. Evidently, when Paul was recounting these events to the Jewish crowd in Acts 22, he chose to connect the Old Testament idea of cleansing in response to prior commitment to God as similar to the baptismal "washing" done while "calling on the name of the Lord." Whatever may be the case, and it is difficult to pinpoint this one verse, the Scripture knows nothing of a "self-baptism" or a "self-washing away of sins." Therefore, that alternative may be ruled out. Neither does the Scripture contain any other verse that would support the normal mode of immersion by someone else as being equal with the mode of "washing away" something.

It is possible that this Acts 22:16 passage refers to the imagery expressed in I Corinthians 12:13 concerning the baptism of the Holy Spirit. That "baptism" places us into the "one body" that belongs to the Lord Jesus. Our sins are certainly washed away when we come to belong to Christ. That picture would be adequate to explain the unusual middle voice construction of the Greek verbs there. That is, "Allow yourself to participate in baptism and allow yourself to participate in the washing away of your sins." Suffice it to say that this verse and this word cannot be proven to be equivalent to the ordinance of baptism, and certainly would create monstrous contradictions with many other passages if they were. Since this is the case, the careful student of the Word will withhold judgment until all other data are examined.

A kindred word is *louo*. And, again, it could have been used by the Holy Spirit to speak of baptism since it carries the meaning of washing the whole body. The Greek Septuagint uses the word to describe the ritual for the preparation of the High Priests for service (Exodus 29:4; Leviticus 8:6; Numbers 19:7), the cleansing of the laver (Exodus 40:10), and the cleansing of defiled persons (Leviticus 11:40; 14:8,9). For this reason, some writers have suggested that *louo* prefigures the New Testament baptismal ordinance, especially since the same word is used in Hebrews 10:22. You remember, that passage notes that we are to come to the Lord "... having our bodies washed with pure water."

However, the context clearly eliminates the possibility of some mystical power connected with water since the passage is drawing a picture of our position as priests before the Lord in the same manner as the priests of the Old Covenant ministered in the tabernacle. Just as their rituals were designed to demonstrate their previous selection and consecration to God, so are we to "enter into the holiest by the blood of Jesus, By a new and living way, which he hath consecrated for us, through the veil, that is to say, his flesh; And having an high priest over the house of God; Let us draw near with a true heart in full assurance of faith, having our hearts sprinkled from an evil conscience, and our bodies washed with pure water" (Hebrews 10:19-22). This passage does not teach baptism.

The other five New Testament references using *louo* refer either to the washing that the Lord Jesus has given us in the forgiveness of sins (John 13:10; Revelation 1:5) or to a physical cleansing from the dirt of a specific environment (Acts 9:37; 16:33; II Peter 2:22). None of these references have anything to do with the ordinance of baptism, although the act of immersion may well be implied. However, since immersion is not necessary for washing oneself, it is interesting to note that the Holy Spirit does not choose to use this word in any passage that clearly talks about the ordinance of baptism.

Nipto is the most frequently used word for

"wash" in the New Testament. However, of the seventeen times it occurs, only one passage can be connected in any way with the baptismal ordinance. The word means "to wash, for the purpose of cleansing, certain portions of the body, normally the hands or feet." The Lord told His disciples to "wash" their faces when they fasted (Matthew 6:17). He told the blind man to "wash in the pool of Siloam" after He had put clay on his eyes (John 9:7,11, 15), and the disciples were told to let Jesus "wash" their feet as the symbol of service for them to follow (John 13:5,6,8,10,12,14). Each of these references and the reference to the faithful widow in I Timothy 5:10 are modal descriptions of a common health practice among the Jews. There is no connection whatever with the ordinance of baptism.

However, in Mark 7:3,5, and 8, the word *nipto* is used in connection with *baptismos* and *baptidzo*, the two words most often used to describe the baptism of the early believers. Therefore, it will be valuable to examine these verses carefully: "For the Pharisees, and all the Jews, except they wash [*nipto*] their hands oft, eat not, holding the tradition of the elders. And when they come from the market, except they wash [*baptidzo*], they eat not. And many other things there be, which they have received to hold, as the washing [*baptismos*] of cups, and pots, brasen vessels, and of tables. Then the Pharisees and scribes asked him, Why walk not thy disciples according to the tradition? .... For laying aside the commandment of God, ye hold the tradition of men, as the washing [*baptismos*] of pots and cups: and many other such like things ye do."

We have to be careful in observing several points in this passage. First, this passage is *not* dealing with the ordinance of baptism. Second, the word usage denotes manner, and manner only. Third, the passage *is* referring to the *perversion* of the Levitical codes. Those codes gave instructions to Israel to wash and/or bathe the priests (Exodus 30:18-21; 40:12,30,31; Leviticus 6:24-27; 16:4,24-28; Numbers 8:5-7; 19:7-10,19-21); and to wash lepers and other sick persons, their clothing, and the articles in the homes after the disease was cured as a sign of cleansing (Leviticus 13:6,34,54,58; 14:8,9,47; 15:5-8,10-16,21-27; 22:6). That code also required a person to wash after touching a dead body (Leviticus 11:25,28,40; 17:15,16), but did not require the legalistic performance that had been set by the Pharisees. This is why the Lord records this example of their error.

However, Mark 7:3-8 does bear on the manner of the ordinance of baptism and is, therefore, important—particularly since the word *nipto* is connected as a synonym to *baptidzo* and *baptismos*. Those who encourage sprinkling or pouring point to this connection, drawing the conclusion that *baptidzo* and *baptismos* are here used in a manner that would not require immersion, especially since "tables" were to be washed. Washing is usually done, they say, by pouring or running water over the object to be washed. Therefore, they conclude, baptism (the ordinance) can be performed in various ways.

Their conclusion is not justified, however, from the information in this passage. During Biblical periods, except for the houses of the very wealthy, there was no "plumbing" or running water. The people drew their water from common springs or wells and stored it in pots and used it for drinking, cooking, bathing, and cleaning. Cleansing was accomplished by using a bowl or tub as a receptacle to hold enough water to allow immersion of the objects to be cleaned, thereby washing away the impurities. The word translated "tables" in Mark 7:4 is the word *kline*, a small cot or portable bed mostly used to carry the sick. It was much the same as our sleeping bag, and could be easily and feasibly washed. Sometimes this "table" was used in the same way that we would use a blanket for a picnic lunch. The people would spread out this "table" and eat off it. That is why the rules had grown so stringent about the "washing" of these various implements. There is no support here for any mode of washing except immersion.

The last three words of this group are *brecho*, *pluno*, and *loutron*. *Pluno* is used only once in the New Testament, but is used several times as the choice of the Greek translators of the Old Testament. The word simply means "to wash," with the implied idea of scrubbing. It is most often used to picture the washing of clothes. *Pluno* is used in Revelation 7:14 where the angel told John that the innumerable multitude surrounding the throne in white robes were those "which came out of great tribulation, and have washed their robes, and made them white in the blood of the Lamb." This obviously has nothing to do with baptism, and since the ordinance of baptism is unknown to the Old Testament, there is little point of examining those verses for such possibility.

Loutron is used only twice. In Titus 3:5, Paul says that "... he saved us, by the washing [*loutron*] of regeneration, and the renewing of the Holy Ghost." In Ephesians 5:26, we are told that the Lord will cleanse the church "... with the washing [*loutron*] of water by the word." Neither of these verses deals with the ordinance of baptism. The Ephesians passage discusses a figurative illustration of the effect that the Word of God has on the righteousness of the Lord's church, and the Titus passage compares the work of the Holy Spirit in salvation to a "bath" of regeneration. That's what *loutron* means: "a bath."

Brecho is used seven times in the New Testament. It is translated "wash" two times, and "rain" five times. The most accurate idea of the word is "to moisten," "to wet," or "to water." Luke records the incident of the repentant harlot who "washed" Jesus' feet with her tears (Luke 7:38,44). The day of judgment will see fire and brimstone "rained" down upon men (Luke 17:29), but God promises to send "rain" as one of His blessings on the just and unjust until then (Matthew 5:45). James notes that Elijah prayed and it did not "rain" for three years (James 5:17), which will also be the case during the time of the "Two Witnesses" recorded in Revelation 11:6. Since none of these passages has any bearing on baptism, they cannot determine the manner of baptizing.

It is worth noting that this word, *brecho*, could have been used to describe the action of sprinkling for baptism if that mode were valid.

Let's regroup our thoughts here. We've covered a lot of ground, and you may feel a little bewildered at the need for all this hard thought process. We've looked at every possible word in the New Testament that could be used to teach us how to baptize. And not one of them has anything to do with that ordinance. Doesn't it strike you as peculiar that the Holy Spirit did not use one of these words—at least once—if He wanted the ordinance of baptism to be administered by sprinkling, pouring, washing, or bathing? He surely used the words to express their ordinary meaning for other things. Why didn't he connect one of those words to "baptize"? Want to know why? Read on!

Chapter 7

Can "Immerse" Be Anything Else?

"Baptize" is a transliteration of a Greek word. A transliteration is a $1.95 way of saying that the translators chose to make a letter-for-letter substitution in the English, instead of substituting the meaning of the word. In this case, the Greek word is *baptidzo*. Just why the translators of the King James Bible chose not to substitute the normal meaning of *baptidzo* is open to some question. Whatever the reason, the translators of every English version since then have continued to render *baptidzo* and its various forms by "baptize" almost every time. This is an interesting habit in light of the large amount of evidence for the word's meaning.

Dr. J. R. Graves, a well-known pastor and editor of the late nineteenth century, published a massive book entitled, *The Great Carrolton*

Debate, which contains his debate with Jacob Ditzler, a Methodist, on the general differences between Baptists and Methodists. The book contains one of the most complete and scholarly discussions of baptism ever published. In it, Dr. Graves quotes from some forty lexicons, all of which give "dip" or "immerse" or "plunge" as the first meaning of *baptidzo*.

After citing these various references, Dr. Graves observes: "The mind that these forty of the most authoritative lexicons extant will not convince, would be as proof against 400. You will notice I have given their definitions in their own words, if in Latin, quoted the text, and that you may decide if I translate properly.... Another fact, every lexicographer of these forty, are paedo-baptist writers, not one a baptist. I therefore submit my argument from the testimony of lexicographers to the public with all confidence."

Most pedobaptist writers (child-baptizers) do not try to defend their positions too strongly from history. In fact, as we have already seen, many of them admit that history supports immersion. However, almost all of those writers insist that *baptidzo* does not always mean immerse. Are they right? If they are, then immersionists are "narrow minded" for insisting that every believer be plunged down into the water and brought out again. Let's investigate.

Baptidzo comes from an earlier word, *bapto*. Many scholars have tried to show that *bapto* does not always mean "immerse," and therefore would leave room for some question and leeway within the meaning of *baptidzo*. Several

Protestant writers and some lexicographers give "wash" as a meaning of *bapto*, and suggest a generic, or more correctly, a ceremonial significance for both *bapto* and *baptidzo*. Alexander Carson, a scholar and pastor of a church in Ireland during the early 1800's, wrote the most extensive book ever attempted on the linguistics of baptism. He covered every use of the words *bapto* and *baptidzo*, in all their forms, throughout all of the classical Greek writings, New Testament writings, and early church writings. His work has never been refuted. It has been ignored, disdained, and treated cursorily, but never disproven. In *Baptism in Its Mode and Subjects*, Carson offered: "The word *bapto*, from which is formed *baptidzo*, signifies primarily to dip; and, as a secondary meaning obviously derived from the primary, it denotes to dye. Every occurrence of the word may be reduced to one or other of these acceptations." Concerning the ceremonial nature of the word, he said, "It has also been said that it is a generic word, and, without respect to mode, or inclusive of all modes, denotes any application of water. So far from this, the idea of water is not at all in the word. It is as applicable to every fluid as to water. Nay, it is not confined to liquids, but is applied to everything that is penetrated. The substance in which the action of the verb is performed, may be oil, or mire, or any other soft matter, as well as water. Except when it signifies to dye, it denotes mode, and nothing but mode."

Dr. Carson also spent a great deal of time reviewing the uses of *bapto* in the Septuagint where there are some 17 uses of the word. Each section is treated independently and shows the word always means "to dip." The one passage in the Septuagint which has frequently been quoted by pedobaptists as showing an example of *bapto* not meaning dip is the passage in Daniel 4:25 where Nebuchadnezzar is said to be "wet" with the dew of heaven.

The observation is usually made that dew is not at all sufficient to immerse a person, and that the imagery would be better satisfied by sprinkling. However, that simply isn't so. Dew is a mist that surrounds the ground as the temperature changes enough to cause condensation of the moisture in the atmosphere. That "dew" is several feet thick, sometimes as much as a hundred feet thick. As the moisture thickens, it sinks slowly to the ground, adding to the moisture level on the ground. Anyone who has spent the night under the stars will know that you really are "immersed" in the dew of heaven. There is no conflict here at all.

In fact, when you examine the overall context of Daniel 4, the picture becomes increasingly clear. The terrible event that happened to Nebuchadnezzar was foretold to him in a dream that was interpreted by Daniel. Later, Belshazzar was reminded of that event by Daniel when Belshazzar had taken over the kingdom. As a result of all this we have four other verses that discuss the same thing. Out of those passages we should be able to establish a sound meaning for the words.

"Nevertheless leave the stump of his roots

in the earth . . . and let it be wet with the dew of heaven . . ." (Daniel 4:15).

"And whereas the king saw a watcher and an holy one . . . and let it be wet with the dew of heaven, and let his portion be with the beasts of the field . . ." (Daniel 4:23).

"The same hour was the thing fulfilled upon Nebuchadnezzar . . . and his body was wet with the dew of heaven, till his hairs were grown like eagles' feathers . . ." (Daniel 4:33).

"And he was driven from the sons of men . . . and his body was wet with the dew of heaven; till he knew that the most high God ruled in the kingdom of men . . ." (Daniel 5:21).

Each of these verses uses the same Chaldean word, *Tseba*. Daniel is the only writer of the Old Testament to use it, and it only appears in these verses. The word means "to dip." There is no disagreement among scholars about the meaning of the word. If you will substitute "dip" for "wet" in each of those verses, you will find that it fits very nicely.

However, in the Greek translation of the Old Testament, the translators chose to use two very different Greek words for this one Chaldean word. In Daniel 4:25, they used *bapto*. Everywhere else they used *aulidzo*. *Aulidzo* means "to lodge in the open, to bivouac." That's a far cry from *bapto*, which means "to dip." Therefore, those who want to find "proof" of *bapto* or *baptidzo* meaning something other than "dip" or "immerse," point to the very different association of these two different Greek words with great enthusiasm. "Here," they say, "is a glaring example of different mode expression and association. The Lord quoted from the Septuagint. So did all the apostles. Evidently they thought it was good enough to use. Surely we can use the Septuagint too, and here is a place where the root word for baptism does not mean immerse. What about that?"

Well, what about it?

Several things. All the emphasis by those who question baptism by immersion is on the Greek Septuagint. That is a translation of another language, just as our *King James Version* is a translation. Translations are made by men. They are not inspired. They are extremely valuable in that they make God's Word available in another language. However, every student of God's Word, in whatever language, must check the *original* language for final answers. The mere fact that translators chose two different words for one original word does not negate the fact that the Holy Spirit chose to use only one word.

Besides that, the words chosen by the Greek translators of the Septuagint do reflect an accurate sense of the context of the passage. The only time *bapto* is used out of the five times where the Chaldean word appears is in Daniel 4:25. That particular verse uses the Chaldean word in a peculiar form that requires Nebuchadnezzar to be placed into the dew of heaven. In that situation, *bapto*, "to dip," was the best choice of Greek words. In the other verses, the Chaldean word is structured so that the emphasis is on Nebuchadnezzar's position in the dew of heaven. That is, the verses describe the *condition* rather than the *action*. In that situation, the Greek word *aulidzo*, "to lodge in the open," is an acceptable descriptive term. It would have been more linguistically correct to have used *bapto* in every case since it directly corresponds to the Chaldean word used by the Holy Spirit. However, the translators chose to use a more pictorial word in the Greek to note the change in emphasis within the verses. There is no support for any meaning for *bapto* except "dip" or "immerse."

Carson also examined many of the medical writings of Hippocrates, and in his book, *Baptism in Its Mode and Subjects*, traces the development of the word *bapto* from its meaning "to dip" to the latter meaning "to dye." He also examined all the forms of the word in the classical writings and the Septuagint. He concluded: ". . . having viewed *bapto* in every light in which it can assist us on the subject . . . I have shown [it] to possess two meanings, and only two, to dip and to dye."

Such stress is given to the meaning of this word in defense against the insistence of those writers who claim the word does not necessarily imply immersion. If the word had any suggestion of pouring or sprinkling, no process could be imagined by which the word would come to mean "dye." Surely it is reasonable to conclude, especially in light of the hundreds of citations from the language use, that *bapto* means to dip under the liquid until the object being dipped is engulfed by the liquid.

After all of that information, it must be observed that *bapto* is never used in connection with the ordinance of baptism. The word appears in Luke 16:24; John 13:26; and Revelation 19:13. A derivative word, *embapto*, is found in Matthew 26:23; Mark 14:20; and John 13:26. All of these usages are translated "dip," and are not even remotely connected with the ordinance of baptism. However, *baptidzo*, which grew out of *bapto*, is used for the ordinance, and must be carefully studied.

Pedobaptist scholars normally teach that since immersionists say that *baptidzo* always means immersion, while history and Scripture show some exceptions, baptism doesn't have to be performed in every instance by putting someone under the water and taking him up again. The pedobaptists' argument doesn't add up, though. Just because the word may not be translated "immerse" every time it appears, it doesn't mean the ordinance may be performed in some way other than immersion.

The word *baptidzo* occurs 80 times in the New Testament—most often in the context of the ordinance of baptism. However, in Mark 7:4 and Luke 11:38 it is translated "wash" and has nothing to do with the ordinance in either place.

A vast amount of work has been done interpreting the classical writers, and the use of the word *baptidzo* is well documented. Carson himself quotes some forty classical writers and some 150 specific passages, all of which are readily seen to mean "immerse" or "engulf" or "plunge" or "overwhelm." All translations clearly signify the imagery of the word, "to immerse." Of the some 150 quotes given to us by Carson, the overwhelming majority are translated "dip," carrying the same meaning that is applied to it today. Other uses are generally figurative, depicting an "overwhelming" or "engulfment" of whatever person, place or thing the writer may be describing. The fact is, there was no other word in the vocabulary of the New Testament Greek writers that would show as strongly and as easily the thought, imagery and drama contained in the ordinance of baptism. For many years prior to the writing of the New Testament, *bapto* and *baptidzo* had been used by scholar and layman alike to give the picture of immersion.

Chapter 8

Are There
Other Immersions?

You have already discovered that only the word *baptidzo* and its derivatives need to be considered in a study of the ordinance of baptism. The word *baptidzo* appears 80 times in the Greek New Testament. The major noun form, *baptisma*, occurs 22 times, and the variant noun forms, *baptismos* and *baptistes*, appear four and 14 times respectively. The classical Greek verb *bapto* is used three times.

It will be possible for us to study the verses using *bapto, baptistes* and *baptismos* rather quickly since they are not used in connection with the ordinance of baptism. The words themselves do bear significance for an identification of the ordinance, but only indirectly through the definition of the words' modal picture. *Bapto* is used only three times: Luke 16:24; John 13:26; and Revelation 19:13. In each instance it expresses mode and is translated "dip" or "dipped." A derivative of *bapto*, *embapto* is used three times: Matthew 26:23; Mark 14:20; and John 13:26. This word is also translated "dipped" each time it is used. John 13:26 uses both words: ". . . He it is, to whom I shall give a sop, when I have dipped [*bapto*] it. And when he had dipped [*embapto*] the sop, he gave it to Judas Iscariot. . . ." Obviously the word is used to show the mode—the kind of action. Not one use of either of these words in the New Testament has a direct bearing on the ordinance of baptism.

The word *baptistes* is used 14 times in the Scriptures: Matthew 3:1; 11:11,12; 14:2,8; 16:14; 17:13; Mark 6:24,25; 8:28; Luke 7:20,28,33; 9:19. In each instance it is used only as part of the name of John the Baptist. The word merely identified this John as the one who baptizes—whatever that is. Again, this word bears no direct relation to the ordinance of baptism except the identifying significance of the word's modal expression. John was called the "Baptist" because he was baptizing. The noun used as part of his name should be translated with the same modal idea as the verb—John the "Immerser." However, that doesn't "sound" right to our twentieth-century ears. One verse, Mark 6:14, uses a specialized form of the verb *baptidzo* as the last name for John. "And king Herod heard of him; (for his name was spread abroad:) and he said, That John the Baptist [*Baptidzon*] was risen from the dead. . . ." Literally, John's name should be translated, "John: the-one-who-is-immersing." This tells us (linguistically at least) that John the Baptist was an immersionist.

Baptismos appears four times in the Scripture. In Mark 7:4,8 it appears twice in a discussion of the Jewish regulations for cleaning certain implements. The other two uses of *baptismos* are in the book of Hebrews. In Hebrews 6:2 the writer is summarizing a rebuke to the Hebrews which he began in 5:12. After bemoaning the fact that his readers were not able to understand, let alone teach, the writer exhorts them to exercise their minds and leave the foundational elements such as "the doctrine of baptisms." Please note that the word is plural. It cannot refer just to the ordinance of baptism since God said there is only one New Testament church baptism (Ephesians 4:5). It could refer to the "baptisms" of "cups, pots, and brasen vessels, and of tables" that we saw back in Mark 7. Or, it could refer to the various "baptisms" of the Lord's suffering, the day of Pentecost, and the baptism into the body of Christ. In Hebrews 9:10 the same Greek word is translated "washings." Neither of these passages has anything to do with the New Testament church ordinance of baptism.

It might be well to briefly summarize the information gained thus far. Every Scripture using the words *bapto*, *baptistes*, and *baptismos* has been examined. None of these Scriptures deals with the ordinance of baptism, nor do any of these Scriptures give proof for any mode of baptism. They do provide some insight into the descriptive nature of the word through the word usage, and that inference seems to be toward immersion rather than toward pouring or sprinkling.

The two remaining words, *baptisma* and *baptidzo*, are used collectively 102 times in the New Testament. Often they are used to speak of the ordinance of baptism. However, let's look at passages in which they do not refer to the ordinance. We need to eliminate these first.

There are seven passages that relate to the baptism of the Holy Spirit: Matthew 3:11; Mark 1:8; Luke 3:16; John 1:33; Acts 1:5; 11:16; and I Corinthians 12:13. Each of these passages uses the English expression, "baptized with the Holy Spirit," except I Corinthians 12:13. The first six passages all deal with the promise of that outpouring of the "Comforter" which would signal the empowering of the work of the Lord's assembly.

John the Baptist preached long and hard about the special "baptism" that the Lord would give. Matthew 3:11; Mark 1:8; Luke 3:16; and John 1:33 all record the same basic message: "I indeed baptize you with water unto repentance: but he that cometh after me is mightier than I, whose shoes I am not worthy to bear: he shall baptize you with the Holy Ghost, and with fire" (Matthew 3:11). Every one of these four verses uses the same Greek words in the English phrase "with the Holy Ghost." However, I feel the word "with" would be better translated "in," from the Greek *en*, especially since it is used in connection with the act of immersing.

The Lord Jesus Himself verified the same

teaching that John the Baptist gave about the baptism *in* the Holy Spirit. In Acts 1:5 He told the apostles of the nearness of that "baptism." Later on, the Apostle Peter quotes the same teaching and the same Greek words in Acts 11:16 where he was talking about the events on the day of Pentecost. If you will read the account of this "baptism" in Acts 2:1,2, you will quickly note that the "sound," which can only be understood as the manifestation of the Holy Spirit, "filled all the house where they were sitting." They were immersed, engulfed, "baptized" *en*, "in," the Holy Spirit. It was *not* a "sprinkling" *by* the Holy Spirit, or *with* the Holy Spirit. It was an immersion *in* the Holy Spirit.

First Corinthians 12:13 is a little different in its teaching. The linguistic construction is basically the same, but the object of the "baptism" seems to be different. In this verse, we are told that we are baptized "into one body." This implies another concept than the very direct words of Acts 2. It is possible that "spirit" here refers to an attitude rather than the Holy Spirit of God, since the Greek word for spirit can mean "attitude" (see I Peter 3:4). But, the start of I Corinthians 12 seems to be talking about the Holy Spirit, not an attitude. That would lead us to believe that verse 13 refers to the Holy Spirit. The Apostle Paul, it seems to me, is telling us that we are "immersed" into one body through the operation of the Holy Spirit.

However, I Corinthians 12:13 could refer back to Pentecost. The Greek words say, "In

[en] one spirit are we baptized. . . ." The emphasis is not on the medium in which we are immersed ("spirit") but the organism into which we are immersed ("body"). Paul's use of the "body" term does *not* establish some new "thing." It is merely an *illustration* of the church of the Lord Jesus Christ. There is a sense in which every Christian is part of the Lord, and there is a sense in which each local church is a complete "body" of the Lord. Both of these applications could be made here. Both of these applications demonstrate the mode of immersion quite clearly, and both of them demand the use of the Greek words *baptidzo* and *en.* No other words would do. However, neither this passage nor these applications have anything to do with the ordinance of baptism. They merely note what *baptidzo* does, not what it is.

In the passages that talk about the "baptism" the Lord Jesus would undergo (Matthew 20:22,23; Mark 10:38,39; Luke 12:50) the words *baptisma* and *baptidzo* are used 13 times. Matthew and Mark simply show that the apostles would share in the "baptism" of the Lord. It is not clear what the "baptism" may be, except that it is not water baptism. Both the apostles and the Lord had already received water baptism. In Luke, the Lord ties the "baptism" with his personal suffering, indicating that the "baptism" may be death itself. These verses could relate to the "baptism" of I Corinthians 12:13, or they could allude to the "death" every Christian experiences with the Lord Jesus at the time of salvation (Galatians 2:20). It is even possible that the Lord is referring to the spiritual "immersion" of the believer into Himself in the same way that He was "immersed" into His peculiar death, burial, and resurrection. Regardless of the theological interpretation of these passages, they do not have anything to do with the New Testament church ordinance of baptism.

Another rather puzzling verse not related to the ordinance of baptism is I Corinthians 15:29. In that marvelous chapter on the resurrection of the dead, Paul presents several arguments to convince the Corinthians of the reality of the coming resurrection of the body. After noting the resurrection of Christ and the promise of eternity with the Lord, Paul wonders why there is a practice of "baptism for the dead" if there is no resurrection.

No one is sure what this practice refers to. Dr. A. T. Robertson, a famous Greek scholar, says that "over thirty interpretations have been suggested . . . no one of which may be correct." The most frequently observed point about this practice is that it is discussed nowhere else in the New Testament, and that it is obvious that the New Testament church did not do it. Most likely the custom was followed by some of the pagan religions in Corinth. There are records of immersion acts taking place in the rites of the temple priests and priestesses which were probably common knowledge. Paul was arguing for the reality of the resurrection by noting that even the pagan world recognized such a reality or else, "Why are they then baptized for the dead?''

We have covered 35 references dealing with the word *baptidzo* and its derivatives. None of these references deals directly with the ordinance of baptism, but all give clear evidence that the words *only* mean immerse. This supports our previous language research. Now we need to check out the passages in the New Testament that do cover the ordinance.

Chapter 9

What is Scriptural Baptism?

The book of Acts gives us the most information about the effort of the first church to baptize, beginning with the great day of empowering by the Holy Spirit on the day of Pentecost. After preaching a stern sermon to the large crowd gathered around the house where they were, Peter responded to the grief of the unsaved people by telling them: "Repent, and be baptized every one of you in the name of Jesus Christ for the remission of sins, and ye shall receive the gift of the Holy Ghost" (Acts 2:38). Then he added a little more to make their need of repentance clear. "Then they that gladly received his word were baptized: and the same day there were added unto them about three thousand souls" (Acts 2:41).

This passage doesn't amplify how they were baptized except to use the word *baptidzo* twice, but it does clearly tell us that everyone who was baptized was old enough to "repent" and to "gladly receive his word."

The next account of baptism is Acts 8:12,13. Philip, one of the deacons from the church at Jerusalem, had gone to Samaria to "preach Christ unto them" (Acts 8:5). The observation is made in verse 6 that the people "gave heed" to Philip—"hearing and seeing the miracles which he did." Finally, after much work, the people began to respond. The Scripture notes: "But when they believed Philip preaching the things concerning the kingdom of God, and the name of Jesus Christ, they were baptized, both men and women" (verse 12). Once again, no specific description is given about how they were baptized except for the use of *baptidzo*. However, a very strong emphasis is made that those being baptized were old enough to give heed; that is, they could reason. And, they "believed"—they exercised personal faith. They were "both men and women," not infants.

The next incident of baptism in Acts occurs in the same chapter, verses 36-39. This section is one of the most explicit passages in the Scripture concerning the ordinance. Philip had been sent into the desert of Gaza by a personal word from the angel of the Lord to meet a eunuch who was traveling back to his home in Ethiopia after having been to Jerusalem to worship. The eunuch was reading from Isaiah 53 and was having a hard time understanding what the prophet meant. Philip offered to help him and "opened his mouth, and began at the same scripture, and preached unto him Jesus. And as they went on their way, they came unto a certain water: and the eunuch said, See, here is water; what doth hinder me to be baptized? And Philip said, If thou believest with all thine heart, thou mayest. And he answered and said, I believe that Jesus Christ is the Son of God. And he commanded the chariot to stand still: and they went down both into the water, both Philip and the eunuch; and he baptized him. And when they were come up out of the water, the Spirit of the Lord caught away Philip, that the eunuch saw him no more: and he went on his way rejoicing."

Notice, the eunuch had to "believe with all his heart" before he could be baptized. This belief was not in the baptism, but rather "that Jesus Christ is the Son of God." Notice, too, that the baptism required an administrator—"both Philip and the eunuch" went into the water. And observe, finally, that the baptism was by immersion—they "went down into the water" and the eunuch was baptized. The strong wording in this passage should eliminate any doubt as to the necessity of prior faith, and the mode of immersion. Faith in Christ precedes baptism by immersion.

Shortly after this event, the Apostle Peter was sent to the house of Cornelius by the Lord to preach the gospel. Peter began his sermon by noting the message of the Old Testament prophets concerning Jesus, and reminded Cornelius that he should be aware that those things were "published throughout all Judaea, and began from Galilee, after the baptism which John preached" (Acts 10:37).

Cornelius, his friends, and his relatives believed on Jesus Christ. They "received the Holy Ghost" and spoke with tongues just as the apostles had on the day of Pentecost. Then they were baptized. When reporting this event to the church at Jerusalem, Peter noted that "the Holy Ghost fell on them, as on us at the beginning" (Acts 11:15).

These three passages of Scripture record the first efforts of the New Testament church after Pentecost to carry out the commission which was given to them just before the Lord ascended to Heaven. All three sections demand believing faith on the part of the one being baptized, prior to baptism, just as had John the Baptist. All three sections consistently use the word *baptidzo* in describing the ordinance's mode, and one passage is so worded that immersion is the only possible description.

But, what do the Scriptures teach about the reason *why* we should be baptized? There is as much confusion about this as there is about the mode.

There are three passages in the epistles of Paul that provide some insight into the reason for the baptismal ordinance. The first of these, Romans 6:3-5, describes what the ordinance pictures. "Know ye not, that so many of us as were baptized into Jesus Christ were baptized into his death? Therefore we are buried with him by baptism into death: that like as Christ was raised up from the dead by the glory of the Father, even so we should walk in newness of life. For if we have been planted together in the likeness of his death, we shall be also in the likeness of his resurrection."

Some Bible teachers suggest that this passage does not apply to the ordinance of baptism at all, but is an amplification of the "baptism" we experience when we are born again. This is possible, but does not seem to be an easy application. Verse 3 uses essentially the same language as I Corinthians 12:13, but adds a new dimension of identity with the death of the Lord. Verse 4 notes that the Christian is buried with Him, and that "like as" Christ rose, the Christian is also to rise and walk in a new life. If the commentary stopped here there would be justification for giving this passage a spiritual interpretation similar to I Corinthians 12:13. However, verse 5 clearly establishes that it is only the "likeness" that Paul is referring to. We may conclude, then, that this whole passage describes the form and figure of the baptismal act.

The form described here is threefold. There is a dying, a burial, and a resurrection. This format is precisely equivalent to the gospel formula given in I Corinthians 15:3,4. The only form of baptism that adequately portrays that formula is immersion. The whole act is performed "on" the subject; that is, he is put down into the water, completely engulfed, and taken back up out of the water. He "dies"— really is "killed" as the Lord was, "buried" and then "raised" just as the Lord was. Both the Christian and the church participate in the reenactment of this unique work of the Lord Jesus.

The Scriptures also contain several passages that discuss the importance of being baptized (immersed) in water. It has already been demonstrated that our Lord recognized the divine credentials behind John's baptizing. John the Baptist was carrying out the will of God by baptizing those who believed his message. It was fitting, therefore, that the Lord Jesus Christ, who always did the will of God, presented Himself to be baptized by John. The Scriptures show, too, that the Lord's disciples, who were baptized by John, began baptizing under the Lord's authority (John 4:2). When our Lord gave the Great Commission, He commanded His apostles to baptize believers. On the Day of Pentecost those commissioned apostles baptized 3,000 who believed the message about Christ (Acts 2:41). Later, deacons were chosen to assist the church in its ever expanding ministry and needs (Acts 6). One of those deacons was Philip. He was used of God to preach Christ to the city of Samaria with great spiritual results. Acts 8:12 tells us that those who believed were baptized. And it was Philip who later led the Ethiopian eunuch to Christ and baptized him (verses 35-39). Peter was called to baptize Cornelius (Acts 10). Paul, or one of his company, having been commissioned by the church at Antioch (Acts 13:1-3), baptized Lydia, the jailer (Acts 16), and others (I Corinthians 1:14-16). Ananias, who was specifically authorized by the Lord (Acts 9:10-18), baptized Paul, who then was taken to the apostles to be examined by the church at Jerusalem. Those twelve disciples at Ephesus, referred to in Acts 19, were required to be properly baptized.

There are very few denominations today that would disagree with the principle that the authority to administer the ordinance derives from the Lord Himself. And it is the responsibility of the local church to administer it to believers. Some church systems might modify that somewhat by suggesting that the church authority is vested in the collective churches, or perhaps, in the action taken by the synods or sessions of the church leaders. However, all church systems are convinced that their particular form and practice is permissible and that it is carried on with proper authority.

What would be the situation if the Lord Himself removed the authority of "churchhood" from a particular church? It is clear from the letters given to the seven churches of Asia (Revelation 2; 3) that the Lord could do so. In fact, He told two of those seven—Ephesus and Laodicea—that He would do just that if they would not repent. In the case of Laodicea the church was morally and doctrinally corrupt. The Lord told that church to "be zealous therefore and repent." But He warned them that their lukewarmness would cause Him to spew them out of His mouth (Revelation 3:16).

The judgment on Laodicea is relatively easy to understand. After all, God cannot abide wickedness, especially when that wickedness is localized in the instrument that He has chosen to bear His Name during this last age. But what about Ephesus? It was a "good" church. The Lord noted how hard its people worked, how much patience they had, "and how thou canst not bear them which are evil: and thou hast tried them which say they are apostles, and are not, and hast found them liars" (Revelation 2:2). Ephesus was a doctrinally sound church that was working hard for the Lord. But . . . they had left their "first love." So the Lord warned them, "Remember therefore from whence thou art fallen, and repent, and do the first works; or else I will come unto thee quickly, and will remove thy candlestick out of his place, except thou repent" (verse 5). That was no idle threat! The risen Lord owns and operates the "candlesticks" (Revelation 2:1) which are representations of the churches (Revelation 1:20). Ephesus was clearly warned to return to their first love or they would be "unchurched."

All of this information raises the question: What would happen to the authority to administer the ordinance if a church were "unchurched" by the Lord? If a church becomes corrupt like Laodicea, like the Roman Catholic system, would God continue to authorize that church to carry His holy name and administer His ordinances? That was precisely the question that drove thousands of churches away from the Roman Catholic system and the various splinter sects of the past centuries. The work of the Lord Jesus Christ was committed by Him to the churches that bear His name and His Word. When those churches become so bad that the Lord cannot tolerate their error, He removes the "candlestick out of his place." When the candlestick is gone, so is the authority.

Our responsibility is to use the ordinance of

baptism in a Scriptural way. According to the New Testament, it is to be administered by immersing a believer in water as a symbol of his union with Christ in His death, burial and resurrection. It is Biblically correct for a church to require baptism of every saved person who wants to become a member of that church. With the obvious importance placed on baptism by the Lord, His apostles, and the early churches of the New Testament, it would clearly be a violation of Biblical doctrine to allow any person to join a church without Scriptural baptism (see James 4:17).

Chapter 10

Can Baptism Save?

As you will recall, one of the dreadful errors connected with the change in baptism was the teaching that baptism had some special power toward salvation. That teaching continues today in some religious groups. Roman Catholicism insists that the baptismal act is necessary for "initial regeneration" and that the remaining sacraments, such as the Lord's Supper, penance, confession, etc., are necessary to continue receiving the grace of God. The various branches of the Disciples of Christ maintain that baptism is the instrument through which salvation is administered, and unless one is baptized he cannot be saved. Many Protestant churches, while not actively promoting such a teaching, do maintain such statements in their creeds and continue to teach the doctrine as "denominational heritage" in the seminaries.

Since this doctrine is so widely held, it seems reasonable that there would be ample Scriptural evidence to support it. Once again, such a study can only be profitable if we are willing to take the Word of God alone as sufficient.

There are four passages that make a direct connection between baptism and repentance, or baptism and salvation: Mark 16:16; Acts 2:38; 22:16; I Peter 3:21. There are four passages that use the phrase "baptism of repentance": Mark 1:4; Luke 3:3; Acts 13:24; 19:4. There are also four other passages that describe a "washing" of sins that may be connected to baptism: I Corinthians 6:11; Ephesians 5:26; Titus 3:5; Hebrews 10:22. And John 3:5 notes that a person must be born of "water." As far as I have been able to determine, these 13 Scripture references are the only ones used by supporters of baptismal regeneration. If we examine these carefully, we should be able to discover what the Scriptures say about this teaching.

Mark 16:16 reads: "He that believeth and is baptized shall be saved; but he that believeth not shall be damned." The Lord had just finished "upbraiding" the apostles because they did not believe the testimony of others about His resurrection. Then He gave the Great Commission to "preach the gospel" (verse 15). That commission is in its complete form in Matthew 28:19,20 where the language requires a proper sequence. "Go ye therefore, and <u>teach</u> all nations, <u>baptizing</u> them in the name of the Father, and of the Son, and of the Holy Ghost: <u>teaching</u> them to observe all things whatsoever I have commanded you." Mark does not depart from the formula, he merely quotes a portion of it.

Obviously, the wording in Mark's passage must be understood as encompassing the whole teaching of baptism *and* salvation. It has already been demonstrated that baptism is a figure of the death, burial, and resurrection of the Lord Jesus, and as such, portrays what takes place in the life of a believer upon salvation—a change that transfers one from death (Ephesians 2:1,5) to a totally new life (II Corinthians 5:17). Mark 16:16 must be understood, then, as viewing a single part of this complex action, even that part which is most obvious to the senses, as being a mention of the whole concept. In other words, the entire change is referred to in language that simply expresses the outward manifestation of the inward transaction. This is frequently done in reference to the ordinance of the Lord's Supper when it is noted only by "the breaking of bread." Only one element is given, the other is assumed.

And, when you understand the importance that is connected with obedience to baptism, it is easy to recognize that there would be ample reason to question whether one who refused baptism really had saving faith. Every record of a salvation experience in connection with the evangelistic ministry of the church shows that the convert was baptized immediately after his salvation. Mark is not teaching that baptism precedes salvation, but that baptism is the immediate response of the saved heart to salvation. The person "believes" and is "baptized." The very next part of Mark 16:16 is, "but he that believeth not shall be damned." If baptism were the key element in salvation, why isn't baptism stated as being required in order to avoid damnation? Obviously, belief is the key—and only belief.

The same basic answer can be given to Acts 2:38: "Repent, and be baptized every one of you for the remission of sins, and ye shall receive the gift of the Holy Ghost." The word order requires that repentance precede baptism. However, some have argued that "remission of sins" is the effect of baptism. According to their view, Peter was saying one had to repent, then be baptized for the real remission. As has already been noted, the element of belief is so strong in this passage that it cannot be denied. To make Peter require baptism for the forgiveness of sins is to deny the instrumentality of the blood of the Lord Jesus. This Peter flatly requires in I Peter 1:18,19. He writes: "Forasmuch as ye know that ye were not redeemed with corruptible things, as silver and gold, from your vain conversation received by tradition from your fathers; But with the precious blood of Christ, as of a lamb without blemish and without spot." Peter didn't believe in baptismal regeneration.

This should be kept in mind in regard to I Peter 3:21, "The like figure whereunto even baptism doth also save us. . . ." Many writers have quoted this portion of the verse in support of baptismal regeneration without quoting the rest: "Not the putting away of the filth of the flesh, but the answer of a good conscience toward God, by the resurrection of Jesus Christ." Obviously, Peter is not teaching that we receive salvation by baptism; he is very careful to make sure that the reader understands this point. He is merely showing that baptism pictures our salvation just as the rescue of Noah and his family pictures the rescue of God's children (verse 20). The Bible does not contradict itself. The "interpreters" often do, but the Bible does not.

Acts 22:16 was discussed at some length earlier in connection with the linguistics of the verse. A repetition of that discussion is unnecessary except to note that it is a summary verse, recalling the entire episode surrounding the meeting of Paul with Ananias. It is clear from both the actual event (Acts 9) and this passage that Paul was saved before Ananias came to him. The imagery of baptism does signify that the sins of the believer have been "washed away." And, as has already been noted, that terminology is applied only to the washing by the blood of the Lord Jesus Christ. As strongly as Paul denounces salvation by any other gospel in Galatians 1:6-9, it is unthinkable that in Acts 22:16 he was giving a testimony that promoted baptismal regeneration. The entire book of Romans refutes such doctrine. Paul did not believe that his salvation was gained through baptism.

The four other verses that are suggested as

proof for the instrumental necessity of baptism in salvation because they speak of a "baptism of repentance" are dismissed on the same basis as the above arguments. Mark 1:4; Luke 3:3; and Acts 13:24 are records of the preaching of John the Baptist. John certainly did not preach that baptism saves.

Acts 19:4 contains the record of the twelve disciples of Apollos who were baptized "unto John's baptism." Paul quickly told them that "John verily baptized with the baptism of repentance, saying unto the people, that they should believe on him which should come after him, that is on Christ Jesus." These men quickly confessed their total ignorance of the person and work of the Holy Spirit. They received instruction and believed the Word Paul declared unto them. They were baptized as Christians and received the Holy Spirit attended by the speaking with tongues.

It should be observed that these Jews had missed Pentecost. Because they were Jewish believers who had missed the apostles' witness, they were given the same experience their Jewish brethren had enjoyed at Pentecost. This was a singular experience, and no Christian today has any right to expect a similar one. Their Christian baptism contributed nothing to their salvation.

The passages that talk about "washing" in one form or another could refer to baptism if it were not for the fact that none of them uses *baptidzo*, which is the key word related to the ordinance of baptism. First Corinthians 6:11's washing most likely refers to the "washing" by the blood of Christ spoken of in Hebrews 10:22.

Hebrews 10:22 specifically reminds Christian people that we may "draw near with a true heart in full assurance of faith, having our hearts sprinkled from an evil conscience, and our bodies washed with pure water." The freedom that we have with our High Priest is based on "faith" and a cleansed "evil conscience." Both of these things are clearly taught in sequence in Scripture: faith, then cleansing or salvation. Baptism follows salvation everywhere in Scripture just as the washing of the bodies follows faith and salvation in Hebrews 10:22.

Titus 3:5 and Ephesians 5:26 have been used for several centuries to justify the use of the baptismal waters as the instrument of salvation. Titus says, "He saved us, by the washing of regeneration, and renewing of the Holy Ghost." Ephesians says concerning the church: "That he might sanctify and cleanse it with the washing of water by the word." In both verses, the word "washing" is a translation of *loutron*, meaning "a bath," or "a bathing." These are the only times the word occurs in the New Testament. According to the Ephesians passage, the "washing" is done "by the word." It is impossible to perform a bathing "by the word" in a physical sense. Therefore the meaning must have some imagery or some spiritual application. It is possible that the foot washing episode recorded in John 13 holds some relationship to the cleansing that we must receive, after we are saved, from the hands of the Lord Jesus. But whatever this passage is referring to, it is *not* referring to the ordinance of baptism.

The Titus passage is even more pronounced in its exclusion of the baptismal ordinance. Paul has just finished recalling to the mind of Titus that "we ourselves also were sometimes foolish, disobedient, deceived, serving divers lusts . . ." when he strongly says to Titus: "Not by works of righteousness which we have done, but according to his mercy he saved us, by the washing of regeneration, and renewing of the Holy Ghost." We are not saved by works (Ephesians 2:8,9; Romans 3:20; 4:4,5). We are saved by the "bath" of regeneration and the "renovation" of the Holy Spirit (II Corinthians 5:17).

The last passage to be considered is John 3:5 which says "Verily, verily, I say unto thee, Except a man be born of water and of the Spirit, he cannot enter into the kingdom of God." These words have been the mainstay of the Roman Catholic teaching for centuries. They have been quoted thousands of times in the liturgies of "baptismal" ceremonies in many Protestant denominations, and are used by the Disciples of Christ as a "proof" of the instrumentality of the baptismal waters in salvation. Why are all these people wrong in applying John 3:5 to baptism?

Well, for one thing, there is such an overwhelming number of passages of Scripture opposing salvation by baptism that it is dishonoring to God's Word to give that interpretation to John 3:5. Furthermore, there is good reason to believe that "water" in John 3:5 refers to the Word of God. This interpretation is based on such passages as John 15:3; I Corinthians 6:11; Ephesians 5:26; and Titus 3:5. Each of these verses may be applied to the cleansing action the Word of God supplies in the work of salvation.

Some Bible teachers explain that the word "and" in John 3:5 joining "water" and "Spirit" may be translated "even." Therefore, they teach that "water" is figurative for the Spirit. Accordingly, the waters of baptism, which symbolize the way a believer enters into the new birth, are representative of the teaching that the Lord is trying to give to Nicodemus. However, the passage has to be somewhat strained to insert a figurative idea, especially when the imagery is adequately explained in the following verse.

A careful examination of the language in John 3:5,6 reveals that the Lord is saying: "Be born [out] of [*ek*] water and [out] of [*ek*] Spirit .... That which is born [out] of [*ek*] the flesh is flesh; and that which is born [out] of [*ek*] the Spirit is spirit." The comparison is absolutely clear. The use of the same preposition (*ek*) and the same verbal case usage, along with the definite articles in verse 6, remove all doubt as to the Lord's meaning in verse 5. In order to "enter into the kingdom of God," one must be born "[out] of water."

This passage does not deal with baptism. It is simply making a clear explanation of the double birth reality. If you are to be a discoverer of "the kingdom of God," you will not only have to be born out of the flesh, but you will also have to be born out of the spirit. Being alive is not enough. Being born into a special family line is not enough. You must be born again!

Not the labors of my hands

Can fulfill Thy law's demands;

Could my zeal no respite know,

Could my tears forever flow,

All for sin could not atone;

Thou must save, and Thou alone.

Chapter 11

Why Do Others Differ?

Those who practice infant baptism frequently support their position by appealing to the five cases in Acts where entire households were baptized. It is doubtful, they say, that these households were made up entirely of adults. Isn't it unreasonable, they ask, to assume that no infants were baptized?

In reply to this argument, we turn first to Acts 10, which records the gathering of Cornelius' "kinsmen and near friends" in his house to hear the Apostle Peter declare "all things that are commanded . . . of God" (see verses 24,33). The account indicates "While Peter yet spake these words, the Holy Ghost fell on all them which heard the word" (verse 44). And the people Peter had brought with him from Jerusalem "heard them speak with tongues, and magnify God" (verse 46). From this account notice that Cornelius' "household" was comprised of "kinsmen and near friends," who "heard the word," "received the Holy Ghost," and "spoke with tongues" *before* they were baptized (verses 47,48).

Another incident involving the baptizing of a "household" is recorded in Acts 16. The Apostle Paul shared the gospel with a group of women at a riverside. Among them was Lydia, "whose heart the Lord opened" (verse 14). The record indicates: "And when she was baptized, and her household, she besought us saying, If ye have judged me to be faithful to the Lord, come into my house, and abide there. And she constrained us" (verse 15). There is no mention of infants being baptized.

Certain things must be noted. Lydia, a businesswoman, was visiting from Thyatira (verse 14). The "household" could have consisted of her servants. At any rate, there is no linguistic reason for insisting that infants were in Lydia's household and were baptized.

The same problem emerges in the case of the Philippian jailer who was led to the Lord by Paul and Silas during a midnight earthquake (Acts 16:25-34). Paul's response to the jailer's request for salvation was, "Believe on the Lord Jesus Christ, and thou shalt be saved, and thy house" (verse 31). Some have suggested that this promises that each of the jailer's children would be immediately saved if the jailer would believe in Christ, but the Scriptures are strongly opposed to this suggestion. Verse 32 says, "They spake unto him the word of the Lord, and to all that were in his house." Everyone in the house—everyone Paul had alluded to in the previous verse—heard "the word of the Lord." The jailer "rejoiced, believing in God with all his house" (verse 34). Infants could not have entered into this experience of joy and faith.

Acts 18:8, another "household baptism" passage, records the simple statement that "Crispus, the chief ruler of the synagogue, believed on the Lord with all his house; and many of the Corinthians hearing believed, and were baptized." This verse refers twice to believing and once to hearing. It does not say unbelieving, incapable-of-hearing infants were baptized. Paul names Crispus along with Gaius and Stephanas.

Finally, I Corinthians 1:16 refers to household baptism. Paul notes that he baptized "the household of Stephanas." No information is given here about the unnamed subjects of baptism, so it seems unsound to demand that they include infants when all other information in the Scripture excludes them.

It is worth noting that some very young children can actually believe and understand, and therefore, would be proper subjects for baptism.

We shouldn't conclude our study of objections to believer's baptism by immersion without answering the issue some teachers raise over Acts 9:18. This verse offers, "[Saul] arose, and was baptized." The argument is that he could not have been immersed, certainly not "buried" symbolically. However, we have already seen that Paul's own retelling of that incident (Acts 22:16) separates the baptizing from the standing. Whatever the case, this passage does *not* say that Paul was sprinkled, rather that he was baptized. The word usage is the sole testimony to mode. We dare not "add" to the words of Scripture.

Some have referred to the Lord's Word in Matthew 19:14 and parallel passages where He says, "Suffer little children, and forbid them not, to come unto me . . ." as supporting infant baptism. However, the children were *not* brought to him for baptism. Matthew 19:13 records, "Then were there brought unto him little children, that he should put his hands on them and pray." There is simply no basis here for infant baptism.

The idea of little children being brought to the Lord for special dedication through baptism has its basis in a teaching that the children of adult Christians are under a covenant of grace in much the same manner as the children of the Old Testament Jews were under a covenant of works. Both of these "covenants" are constructs of theologians. Neither term appears in the Scripture, but rather is developed by the various implications within the two major divisions of the Bible. It is true that the Old Testament saints operated under a different "covenant" than we do, and that the main distinction between the two "covenants" was the law of Moses. But it is not true that the Old Testament saints were saved by any other means than the grace of God. Romans 4 makes it clear that faith in God's Word secured salvation—just as it does today.

Many non-immersionist theologians support that point, but insist that there is a physical connection to the people of God in much the same manner as there was in the nation of Israel. Much of the Old Testament describes God's working to bring about the birth of the Messiah through the "peculiar people," the Jews. They were given special laws designed to make an observable distinction between Israel and all other nations (Leviticus 20:22-26). One of those laws required circumcision. So many writers compare circumcision to baptism. That is, baptism is the sign of the New Covenant just as circumcision was the sign of the Old Covenant. Circumcision and baptism are both to be applied to the children of the adult covenant members.

There is a sense in which that application may be correct. Colossians tells us that baptism is the "circumcision of Christ" (Colossians 2:11,12). However, there is a vast difference between the identification factors of circumcision and the identification factors of baptism. It would be strained to insist on baptism's application to infant children, in spite of the Scriptural evidence to the contrary, merely because baptism is the New Covenant "sign."

Circumcision was performed only on the male children of Israel because the Old Covenant was directed to the promise of the coming *seed* of Abraham. Baptism identifies with both sexes, all nations, and all classes with the *work* of the Lord Jesus Christ. Circumcision was an intensely *private* matter, being primarily a sign to the individual concerned, his parents, and his wife. Baptism is a *public* matter, to be performed in open testimony of the individual's new birth. Circumcision was an *involuntary* act, perpetrated on the individual without his consent or knowledge. Baptism is a *conscious* act, answering, as Peter says, with "a good conscience toward God" (I Peter 3:21). Circumcision was to be done *prior* to the individual's opportunity to prove himself worthy of the covenant. Baptism is only to be administered *after* there is evidence of repentance and faith (Acts 2:38-41). There is no similarity between the signs of the two covenants. Their only common ground is the purpose of marking the covenant people.

These several problems, household baptism, Paul's baptism, and the covenant relationship are not defensible from Scripture alone. One may well build a case on the basis of logic, but if logic contradicts the words of God, then "let God be true and every man a liar" (Romans 3:4).

Chapter 12

How Firm
Can We Be?

We need to correlate the points of solid evidence that we have obtained from this research. Each major area has produced information, which of itself is worth considerable weight in considering the ordinance of baptism. However, no one area has enough evidence to "prove" one mode or one practice above the other. The Scriptures definitely show that immersion was performed on knowledgeable believers after salvation. But, you could argue that the Scriptures do not expressly forbid the sprinkling of infant children. The language of Scripture definitely shows that only one unique word is employed by the Holy Spirit to describe the mode of the ordinance. But, you could argue that the churches have practiced other modes for centuries, and, since God has blessed those churches, the words used must merely be a record of the prevalent mode of Jewish practice, not demanding on the New Testament church. History records that the initial practice of the early church was in accord with Scripture. But you could argue that the early church was of necessity only composed of adults, and that as history progressed, the church would incorporate the covenant families into its membership through baptism. Therefore, it is possible to skirt one or two areas of information if you want to. But, when taken together, these three areas of evidence present a tremendously solid wall of data.

The historical evidence provides the following facts:

1. Sprinkling was known in the second century, but immersion was the majority practice until well into the fifth and sixth centuries.

2. Infants were not permitted baptism until the third century, and were predominantly refused baptism until the seventh and eighth centuries.

3. The twin doctrinal errors of church hierarchy and baptismal regeneration were formed in the first and second centuries, giving rise to the change in both the mode and the subject of baptism.

4. Many churches refused to accept the authority of the emerging Roman

Catholic church system because it departed from the practice of immersion and performed infant baptism.

5. There was strong resistance to the changes of doctrine and practice within the Rome-centered church system, even on the part of those churches that eventually combined with the state.

6. There were millions of people in thousands of churches throughout every century who did not follow the lead of the Roman Catholic system.

7. Those churches who refused to identify with Rome were all marked by three distinct doctrines: the Scriptures were to be the sole rule of faith and practice; the ordinances were not sacramental in nature, and baptism was to be performed by immersion upon a believer who had given evidence of personal faith in the work of the Lord Jesus; each church was to be autonomous and separate from the state.

All of these factors can be summarized into two conclusions. First, the churches of early history have demonstrated that the immersion of believers was considered to be the teaching of the Scriptures. Second, when some churches began to change the mode and the subject, most churches fought against such changes at the peril of their lives. This question must now be answered by supporters of pedobaptism: Why did God's people resist the changes so vehemently if the changes were permitted by Scripture?

The linguistic evidence provides the following facts:

1. The words of Scripture which mean "sprinkle" or "pour" are not used in any passage that is connected to the ordinance of baptism.

2. The words of Scripture which mean "wash" or "bathe," although used in some passages where the idea of immersion is necessary, are never used in connection with the ordinance of baptism.

3. The Scriptures use the verb *baptidzo* and the noun *baptisma* only in passages dealing with the ordinance of baptism.

4. All lexicons give "immerse" or "dip" as the first and primary meaning of both words, and demonstrate that those words are modal words only.

5. An examination of the appearances of *baptidzo*, *baptisma*, and their root word, *bapto*, show that the meaning of those words has remained the same for centuries. And, that the meaning is always modal, expressing the total engulfment of the object being "baptized."

All of these factors lead the student to one inescapable conclusion. The Scriptures use only one verb and one noun for conveying the meaning of *baptism*. That meaning is *immersion*. Aspersionists must deal with that fact.

The Scriptural evidence exhibits the following facts:

1. The passages that contain the verb *bapto* do not relate to the ordinance of baptism.

2. The noun *baptistes* is used only as the last name for John the Baptist, and is related to the ordinance only as it describes what John was doing.

3. Those passages that use the noun *baptismos* deal only with the description of the Old Testament washings, and do not relate that Old Testament concept to the New Testament ordinance of baptism.

4. The symbolism of baptism is a portrayal of the death, burial, and resurrection of the believer in the same likeness as the Lord Jesus Christ in His work for the believer's salvation.

5. The authority to baptize is vested in the Lord Jesus Christ Himself, who has granted this authority to His churches. When a church becomes apostate, it no longer has the authority to baptize.

6. The problem of "household" baptism, the

covenant relationship, and the unique-
ness of Paul's baptism are not Scriptur-
ally supportive of infant or aspersion baptism.

7. Baptismal regeneration is not taught by
Scripture.

These several factors all demonstrate with
clarity and strength that baptism, as a church
ordinance, must be conducted by the immersion of a believing Christian in water upon confession of his faith and evidence of his repentance for the purpose of signifying to all the
world his identification with Christ in His
death, burial and resurrection.

Individually, these conclusions may leave
room for debate. Collectively, however, they
demand obedience. The Scriptures teach only
one doctrine of baptism. There is no support
for other modes or other subjects. The language used demonstrates that the Holy Spirit
was precisely consistent with the doctrine by
using only the word that must mean *immerse*.
History verifies the truth of these points by
recording the resistance to departure from the
Scriptural teaching, and by recording the
voices of protest still ringing out against the
error. To deny these facts is to deny reality.
To refuse the application of these facts is to admit unwillingness to love truth. The God of
Heaven holds every Christian responsible for
his treatment of truth. The unsaved have no
way of relating to the significance of obedience,
and can see no reason for the seriousness of

God's Word when there is indifference or disobedience on the part of God's people. The Lord has commanded His churches to baptize every disciple. The Scriptures have clearly spoken about the procedure. The churches of history have demonstrated allegiance to the Scripture. What will you do?